Bougainville Island

Early History, First European Contact, German Period, World War II, Civil War, People and Culture, Island Information

Author
Victor Ross

Copyright Notice

Copyright © 2017 Global Print Digital
All Rights Reserved

Digital Management Copyright Notice. This Title is not in public domain, it is copyrighted to the original author, and being published by **Global Print Digital**. No other means of reproducing this title is accepted, and none of its content is editable, neither right to commercialize it is accepted, except with the consent of the author or authorized distributor. You must purchase this Title from a vendor who's right is given to sell it, other sources of purchase are not accepted, and accountable for an action against. We are happy that you understood, and being guided by these terms as you proceed. Thank you

First Printing: 2017.

ISBN: 978-1-912483-01-3

Publisher: Global Print Digital.
Arlington Row, Bibury, Cirencester GL7 5ND
Gloucester
United Kingdom.
Website: www.homeworkoffer.com

Table of Content

- Introduction 1
- History 3
  - *History in more Detial* 15
    - The First 28,000 Years 15
    - First Contacts with Europeans 33
    - The German Era 63
    - Mandated Territory 88
    - World War II 152
      - The Post-War Era 170
  - *The Mine* 176
- **Bougainville Beyond Being** 191
  - *Conflict and Peace* 192
  - *The Impacts of Change* 194
  - *Identity and Separatism* 195
  - *The Importance of Custom* 200
  - *Future Governance in Bougainville* 204
- **Bougainville Struggle: independence and the mine** 207
- **The People, Culture, Tradition and Festivals** 216
  - *Reeds Festival* 216

Introduction

Bougainville is politically an autonomous region within Papua New Guinea (PNG), but geographically a part of the Solomon Islands Archipelago. It is the biggest island in the north of the Solomons chain and is a mere eight kilometres from the sea border of the independent state of the Solomon Islands. Bougainville has been colonised and invaded a number of times over the past few hundred years. The history, including the development of the Panguna mine, is set out in Bougainville: the long struggle for freedom by the late Moses Havini.

Since at least the 1960s, Bougainville's economy and politics have been dominated by mining of its significant mineral resources, which led to the devastating 'Bougainville Crisis' of the 1990s.

In 2001 a Peace Agreement was negotiated between PNG and representatives of Bougainville groups, providing for autonomous government, a referendum on independence, and a weapons disposal plan. This was followed by the enactment of the Autonomous Region of Bougainville Constitution and the election of the inaugural Autonomous Bougainville Government (ABG) in 2005. Further general elections were held in 2010 and 2015.

History

The Solomon Islands nation lies immediately to the southeast of the Papua New Guinea island of Bougainville, separated by a narrow strait. Bougainville is the largest island in the Solomons Archipelago. Twenty-eight to eighteen thousand years ago, when seas levels were lower, Bougainville was the north of a single land mass that included Buka, Shortland Islands, Choiseul, Isabel and Nggela. Bougainvilleans are close relatives of Solomon Islanders to the south, particularly those of the Western Solomons.

The 168 islands in the present-day Autonomous Region of Bougainville cover 9,300 square kilometres, with Bougainville and Buka being the main islands (250 kilometres north-south). There are also a number of small islands (many uninhabited), island groups and atolls, including Nissan (Green), Nuguria (Fead), Takuu (Mortlock), Nukumanu (Tasman) and Tulun (Carteret). Bougainville is home to several active and dormant volcanoes, and central mountains rise to 2,400 metres.

Mt. Bagana in the north-central part of Bougainville is extremely active and overall volcanic activity has created a coastal plain of rich volcanic soil. Bougainvilleans stress matrilineal descent, which sets them apart from many other Papua New Guineans. They are dark-skinned, far darker than other Papua New Guineans but similar in skin-colour to their neighbours in the Western Solomons. (Friedlaender 2005)

Human occupation of Buka Island, contiguous with north Bougainville, dates back thirty-two thousand years, the earliest date for human settlement in the Solomon Archipelago. Three or four thousand years ago a significant new group of migrants, agriculturalist Austronesians, arrived from Asia via the north coast of New Guinea and the Bismarck Archipelago, bringing with them domesticated pigs, dogs, and chickens, as well as obsidian tools, and they settled alongside the earlier inhabitants. (Spriggs 2005) Bougainville has many languages, both Austronesian and Papuan (Non-Austronesian).

The most widely spoken of the seventeen Austronesian languages is Halia and its dialects, spoken in Buka, Kilinailau (Carteret) and the Selau Peninsula in northern Bougainville. Other Austronesian languages-Haku, Petats, Solos, Saposa (Taiof), Hahon, Piva, Banoni, and Tinputz (Vadoo), Teop, Papapana, Torau (Rovovana), Urava (now extinct), Nehan, Takuu, Nukumanu and Nuguria-were spoken on Buka, outlying islands and atolls and several parts of Bougainville. Nine Papuan languages are spoken on the main island: Kunua (Konua), Rotokas, Eivo, Keriaka, Nasioi (Kieta), Telei (Buin), Nagovisi, Motuna (Siwai), and Buin (Telei). (Tryon 2005)

Because of its size and fertility Bougainville probably always has been the most populous of the Solomon Islands, followed by Malaita and Guadalcanal. The pre-contact population of Bougainville, Buka and the surrounding outliers could easily have been one hundred thousand and possibly higher, even allowing for malaria limiting the size of the population. Significant depopulation took place on all Solomon Islands during the nineteenth century (q.v. Demography).

The first British Solomon Islands Protectorate census in 1931 recorded a total of 94,066 people, but the Protectorate's pre-contact population was probably in excess of two hundred thousand and possibly twice or even three times that number, and this has implications for trying to calculate the size of Bougainville's early population. In 1914 the Germans estimated its population at around 32,000. Australian estimates were 36,000 in 1931, 41,000 in 1935, 51,190 in 1940, around 50,000 in 1942, 59,250 in 1967 and 129,000 in 1980. (Nelson 2005; Lummani 2005) The population of the Autonomous Region of

Bougainville in 2000 was 175,160. (Turner 2001) These numbers are similar to the population of Malaita during these decades.

European voyages began to pass by Bougainville in the seventeenth century: Schouten and Le Maire in 1610, Tasman in 1643, Carteret in 1767 and Bougainville in 1768. As in other parts of the Solomons and the Bismarck and Louisiade Archipelagos, in the first half of the nineteenth century whalers and traders worked around Bougainville and Buka, and the New Britain-based Forsayth company recruited labour and purchased copra on Nukumanu and the Mortlocks in the 1870s and 1880s. Thirty-three indentured labourers left Bougainville, Buka and Nissan for Queensland in the 1870s, followed by another 278 in the 1880s. (Price with Baker 1976) Over the same years 710 labourers from these islands went to work in Fiji. (Siegel 1985)

The original 1884 declaration of German New Guinea (q.v.) was vague on its eastern extreme because the status of the Solomon Archipelago was unclear. In 1886 Bougainville was proclaimed part of German New Guinea when the eastern border was defined as including Buka, Bougainville, the Shortlands, Choiseul, Isabel and Ontong Java. Britain claimed the remainder of the Solomon Archipelago as a Protectorate in 1893. Then in 1899-1900 another Anglo-German convention shifted the German-British border north to between the Shortlands and Bougainville.

Bougainville Strait became the dividing line and the peoples of southern Bougainville found themselves politically divided from their close kin in the Shortlands and on Choiseul. Powerful Shortlands chiefs such as Gorai, son of Porese, helped the Protectorate traders obtain coconuts from Bougainville, and traders never felt bound by the border, crossing at will. The first official tours of inspection of the German North Solomons were made in 1888, 1893 and 1900, searching for a suitable place to establish a government station.

Once the Catholics established a base at Kieta, this was chosen as the most suitable government base. (Sack 2005) After recruiting to Queensland and Fiji ceased, North Solomons labourers were absorbed onto German plantations. Between 1907 and 1913, 5,214 Bukas and Bougainvilleans were recruited by the Germans and others crossed from southern Bougainville to work in the Shortlands. During the German years (until 1914), Bougainville was primarily a labour reserve along with the beginnings of a local plantation economy.

The first plantation, at Kieta in 1902, was a side-product of the Marist mission. The first fully commercial plantation was established by the Bismarck Archipel Gesellschaft at Aropa in 1908 and another was begun by the New Britain Corporation at Toiemonapu two years later. By 1911 there were ten plantations on Bougainville, with another ten thousand acres recently acquired by Hernsheim and Co., which also had trading branches in Kieta, Buin, Petatz, Arawa and Enus. Just before the Germans lost control, Lever Brothers applied to the governor to extend their Solomon Island plantation interests into Bougainville. The non-indigenous population of the Northern Solomons remained low, at seventy-four in 1914, one-third of them part of the Marist mission. (Sack 2005; Bennett 2000)

Initial missionary work on Bougainville came from the Catholics (q.v.) and Methodists (q.v.), as part of endeavours that reached out of the British Solomon Islands and across Bougainville Strait. The Catholic Society of Mary (Marist) missionaries began a new phase of Catholic outreach to the Solomons in 1898. From their base in the Shortland Islands in 1901, Marists established their Kieta base and soon after used the close trading and kin links between the Shortlands and southern Bougainville to establish a base at Patupatuai on the Buin coast, making patrols further inland.

Between 1901 and 1922, when their mission monopoly was broken, the Marists established several stations between Burunotui on Buka and Patupatuai. Between 1901 and 1939 eighteen Marist stations were established on Bougainville and Buka. The South Solomons prefecture was elevated to an apostolic vicariate in 1912 (including Guadalcanal, Makira and Malaita) with the same elevation granted to the North Solomons in 1930 (Buka and Bougainville). Thomas Wade, an American, became the first bishop of North Solomons. (Laracy 2005a, 2005b)

After a brief sojourn in 1916 at Siwai, the Methodists arrived permanently on Bougainville in 1922, establishing a base in Siwai, and incurred a great deal of resentment from the Marists. Like the original Catholic mission, the Methodist's Bougainville venture was an extension of their work in the Western Solomons. The Methodists were firmly established on New Georgia by 1914 and began to cast their eyes toward Bougainville. They succeeded in establishing themselves on Mono, the main Treasury Island, which had close trading and kin alliances with Bougainville.

After Australia seized German New Guinea in 1914, the Methodists felt secure enough to expand into Bougainville. In 1916, Methodist boundaries were altered to include the German Solomons into the New Georgia district. The border at Bougainville Strait did not stop the constant indigenous movements nor the movement of mission personnel, although by the 1920s discussions were held to try to stop

Buin labourers working in the Protectorate. (Bennett 2000) Seventh-day Adventists (q.v.) were also active in the Western Solomons, following the Catholics and Methodists to Bougainville. In 1924, R. H. Tutty and two Solomon Islander evangelists, Nano and Rongapitu, sailed to Lavilai on Bougainville and established a station there. In 1927, A. J. Campbell worked for some months on Bougainville, and the next year the first two local converts were baptized there. Today, seventy percent of people in the Autonomous Region of Bougainville are Catholics.

In an early act of the First Wold War Australian armed forces arrived on 9 December 1914 and took control of Bougainville, and a final transition to Australian administration was made in 1921 once the League of Nations Mandate was enacted. By the 1920s large coastal areas in Buka, and along the north, south and east coasts of Bougainville had become coconut plantations. Labour was mainly from Bougainville and Buka. The administration remained based at Kieta. German plantations and other property were disposed of via an Expropriation Board, with Germans only able to claim compensation from their own government.

The plantations were reserved for Australian servicemen who had served in the First World War, an extension of the soldier-settler experiment in Australia. Police patrols were concentrated around Kieta and a police post was established at Kangu near Buin on the south coast in 1919, although regular patrols did not begin in the south until the mid-1930s. The small hamlets which had dominated the earlier settlement pattern were discouraged by the administration in favour of larger ordered villages. Burns Philp, through its subsidiaries and Choiseul Plantations Ltd., became the largest managers of plantations, and W. R. Carpenter & Co. Ltd. Was also involved in trading and plantation management. (Elder 2005; MacWilliam 2005)

In 1942 the Australian administration and most of the planters and missionaries fled before the Japanese advance, just as most whites did in the British Solomons. During the Second World War (q.v.) parts of Bougainville were under Japanese control between January 1942 and August 1945. Initially the Japanese numbers on Bougainville were small and they were not in direct contact with the Australians who had remained. Then from August 1942 to July 1943 coastwatchers (q.v.) were able to give advance warning of Japanese ships and planes heading south into the Solomons.

The Japanese dominated Bougainville in mid-1943, but then between November 1943 and October 1944 the Americans began to fly there, and onwards from October 1944 Australian troops were responsible for the island's recapture. Around forty thousand Japanese, two thousand Allies and an unknown number of Bougainvilleans (probably around 16 percent) died during the war. (Nelson 2005)

In 1945, once the war was over, the islands returned to Australian control. War damage took a decade to repair, but slowly the plantations began to operate again. Burns Philp worked hard to re-establish their plantations, and plantations diversified to interplant coconut palms and cocoa trees, the new crop of the 1950s. Official development policy changed to include Bougainvilleans as smallholders and co-operative societies were established. Village-made copra and cocoa began to enter the market, creating a small indigenous bourgeoisie. Between the 1960s and 1980s most Bougainvilleans turned to cocoa and coconuts as their dominant cash crops, although production plummeting in the 1990s during the civil war. (MacWilliam 2005; Lummani 2005)

In 1964 a large copper deposit was discovered at Panguna on Bougainville by a subsidiary of Conzinc Riotinto Australia. Mining at Panguna, which became the second largest open cut mine in the world, began in 1969 with the first exports in 1972. The mining agreement was made between Bougainville Mining Company, later

Bougainville Copper Ltd. (both CRA subsidiaries) and the Australian administration, ratified by the House of Assembly in Port Moresby, with little consultation with or compensation of the landowners. Australia saw the huge copper mine as a way to provide finance for the approaching independent government of Papua New Guinea. This uneven agreement sowed the seeds for the conflict that occurred in the 1980s and 1990s. (Vernon 2005; Denoon 2000)

There had been many suggestions during the first half of the twentieth century that the North Solomons be reunited with the British Solomon Islands Protectorate, or that the Protectorate be combined with Papua New Guinea, but all failed to eventuate. During the 1950s and 1960s, Bougainvilleans were unhappy about their future as part of Papua New Guinea. They always regarded themselves as different from other Papua New Guineans and identified more closely with the rest of the Solomon Islands, based on their dark skin colour and matrilineal societies, and also their geographic isolation from the other islands off eastern New Guinea.

Bougainvilleans rightly regarded the Panguna mine agreement as exploitative and grew to fear the environmental damage being caused by the mine. The first moves for succession were in 1964, extended by the exploitative mining agreement and unwillingness to join with the rest of Papua New Guinea at independence in 1975. (Griffin 2005) Discontent simmered with Bougainvilleans in the National Parliament being strong advocates for devolution of power to the provinces. In 1988 a rebellion began which became a protracted civil war.

The rebel Bougainville Revolutionary Army (BRA) was formed, forcing the mine to close in 1989, with a civilian government established under Francis Ona. Between 1990 and 1994 the PNG Defence Force fought the BRA. In 1991, a Bougainville Interim Government was established, which in 1995 became the Bougainville Transitional Government (BTG).

The PNG government calamitously tried to bring in mercenaries (O'Callaghan 1999; Dorney 1998), and finally a permanent cease-fire was established and an unarmed peace-monitoring group was created staffed from Australia and New Zealand, Vanuatu and Fiji. In 1997 an Autonomous Region of Bougainville was agreed to, still within Papua New Guinea but with provision for future independence.

There was an election in 1999 in which Joseph Kabui, commander of the BRA, was elected president of the BTG; he died in June 2008 and was succeeded by John Tabinaman as acting president. Since December 2008, James Tanis has been president. Frances Ona died in 2005. The peace agreement that was finalised in 2000 was brokered with the help of New Zealand. There will be a future referendum on whether the Autonomous Region of Bougainville will become an independent nation. (Turner 2001)

The crisis in Bougainville impacted the Solomon Islands since supplies including guns and ammunition that passed over the border, and Bougainvilleans used health facilities as far south as Malaita and Honiara. The Bougainville crisis also gave some momentum to the internal crisis between Malaita and Guadalcanal in the late 1990s.

History in more Detial
The First 28,000 Years

The first humans to set foot on Bougainville-Buka, some 28,000 years ago, came from the northwest - either directly, from southeastern New Ireland or, more probably, by stages from there via the Feni and Nissan Islands. The present open-sea distances between New Ireland and Buka, via Feni and Nissan, are no wider than 72 kilometres. Their coasts may have been even closer during the Pleistocene period, when the sea level throughout this area had been low3ered appreciably as a result of the impounding of much of the earth's waters in vast continental ice sheets. But even 72-kilometre stretches of ocean were well within the seafaring range of these pioneers: their canoes were certainly seaworthy enough, and the inter-island distances sere within visibility range (Lewis 1972).

There is no mystery about how the ancestors of those pioneers came to be in New Ireland at that early date. Archaeological evidence from both New Guinea and Australia (which were periodically joined together during low-sea-level phases of the Pleistocene) shows that humans had begun to cross over from insular Indonesia as early as 50,000 years ago, and that some of them had spread eastward into New Britain and New Ireland by about 30,000 years ago.

It is also quite likely that some of the early descendants of the first Bougainvillians pressed further southeastward, at least as far as the island of San Cristobal. There is no means of knowing why those pioneers made their ways to Bougainville, or beyond: escape from victorious enemies? deliberate search for richer food supplies? need for safe landings during stormy fishing expeditions? or perhaps, in a few cases, curiosity about unfamiliar shores?

More certain is how they subsisted. From archaeological evidence it can be inferred that their diet consisted of forest vegetables, fish and shellfish, birds, lizards, fruit bats, and rats. Included among the vegetables they gathered and ate were two species of taro, *Colocasia* and *Alocasia*, some of which may have been 'tended' (i.e., semi-domesticated) long before the indigenes began to cultivate them in gardens. For some 25,000 years after initial settlement, the Bougainvillians appear to have had little contact with their northwestern homelands, except, for example, for their import of the galip nut (*Camarium indicus*), which they proceeded to plant and use as a favoured food supplement.

Even opossums (*Phalanger orientalis*), which were to become highly favoured hunting prey, did not reach Bougainville-Buka un til 3200 years ago. Thus, the first Bougainvillians were to remain almost entirely isolated from their northwestern homelands for nearly twenty-five millennia. although they were isolated, they were evidently not unified, and most certainly not homogenous, either physically or culturally.

During those many millennia, the pioneers' descendants proliferated and dispersed, mostly in the larger island, where indigenous terrestrial food resources were richer and more diverse. In time those little bands of food gatherers and hunters (and in some places, fishermen), dispersed so widely and remained so scattered that they evolved into many, sharply different, societies, each with its own language.

(A society as herein defined is a social unit composed of people who reside adjacently, speak the same language, or languages, and who share, in large measure and more or less distinctively, a common set of cultural principles, values, and practices. In some parts of Melanesia a single community constituted a whole society as well, but in most cases a society contained two or more communities.) Some of those earlier languages may in the course of time have died out, but in the year 1939 there were nine of them:

Northern stock	Southern stock
Rotokas family	Nasioi family
1. Rotokas proper	5. Nasioi
2. Eivo	6. Simiku
3. Kunua	7. Nagovisi
4. Keriaka	Terei family
	8. Buin
	9. Siwai

This classification is based mainly on the degree of similarity between the languages' vocabularies. In addition there are some significant differences between the northern and southern stocks with respect to grammar. For example, the languages of the southern stock classify their numerals into forty or more categories, according to the nature of the objects they count; the northern languages lack such a classification but share a complicated kind of verbal system that differs markedly from the one found in those of the south.

Linguists have not yet calculated how long the two stocks have been separated, but clearly it must be reckoned in thousands of years. During this time there developed several other marked differences between the cultures of the northern and southern societies (including cannibalism and male initiation rites in the north but not in the south).

On the other hand, both northerners and southerners retained their common practice of affiliating individuals into matrilineal clans - supra-familial social units made up of persons related by maternal, rather than than paternal, kin ties. This is evidently a cultural heritage of their common ancestry from New Ireland and New Britain, where such matriliny also prevails.

Another trait shared by the present-day descendants of both northerners and southerners is their skin colour, which is very black. Indeed, it is darker than that of any population of present-day Pacific islanders, including the present-day indigenes of New Ireland, the larger homeland of the first Bougainvillians.

The presence of Bougainville as a 'black spot' in an island world of brownskins (later called redskins) raises a question that cannot now be answered. Were the genes producing that darker pigmentation carried by the first Bougainvillain s when they arrived? Or did they evolve, by natural or by 'social' selection, during the millennia in which the descendants of those pioneers remained isolated, reproductively, from neighbouring islanders? Nothing now known about Bougainville;s physical environment can support an argument for the natural selection of its peoples' distinctively black pigmentation; therefore a case might be made for social selection, namely, an aesthetic (and hence reproductive) preference for black skin. This preference has, by the way, surfaced recently with added political meaning.

While alike in their distinctive skin colour (and in the Melanesia-wide frizziness of their hair), the descendants of Bougainville's pioneer settlers eventually became differentiated into two major types with respect to some other bodily traits: a taller and broader northern type, and a shorter, slenderer southern one. This distinction corresponds to the language differences noted earlier.

Bougainvolle's long-lasting isolation was not ended until about three to four thousand years ago. Then, people having different physiques, speaking entirely different kinds of languages, and bearing many cultural innovations, surged from the west into the Pacific and on into or through New Britain, New Ireland, the Solomons and the New Hebrides. (From the Solomons some of the descendants of these newcomers moved on into the Gilbert Islands, and thence on to the Marshalls and Carolines.

From the New Hebrides others moved into Fiji and Tonga and Samoa, where they evolved into the people now known as Polynesians.) Meanwhile, beginning about 3200 years ago, some bands of those newcomers settled on Buka and on Bougainville's northern and southwestern coasts. Much later, the descendants of some of those who had settled on the islands immediately south of Bougainville, resettled along Bougainville's eastern coast; the most recent of these movements founded the present-day community of Roruana, only about a century ago.

The descendants of the newcomers who settled on Buka and on the fringes of northern Bougainville eventually superseded or mixed with whatever firstcomers still remained there, as revealed by the entirely different kinds of languages spoken there today. These newer languages are all interrelated and they are as different from the earlier ones as is, say, English from Arabic. They are divided into two groups (see Figure 3); one consisting of Tinputz, Teop, and Hahon; the other of Petats, Halia, Solos, and Saposa. All of these newcomer languages are members of a vast family of languages labelled Austronesian, which originated in south China and/or Formosa. Austronesian languages proliferated and spread throughout Southeast Asia (with one branch in far-off Madagascar) and all over the Pacific.

They are found in the islands of Micronesia and Polynesia, and of Melanesia, except for most of New guinea and pockets of earlier, non-Austronesian languages elsewhere, including those of Bougainville. (In the connection, some linguists believe all or most of Melanesia's non-Austronesian languages to be members of a single, 'genetically' interrelated group which they label *Papuan*, but expert opinion is not unanimous on this point.)

As Figure 3 shows, Austronesian languages are spoken also on Bougainville's central coasts, both east and west. Banoni and closely related Nagarige-Amun, spoken on the west coast, are direct and fairly recent offshores of the island's northern Austronesian languages; on the east coast Torau (also called Roruana) and Papapana are spoken by people whose ancestors migrated there from the Shortland Islands only a few generations ago.

When the author was on Bougainville in 1938-9 the present site of the town of Arawa was occupied by a small community speaking an Austronesian language also derived from the Shortlands at a time somewhat earlier than the arrival of the speakers of Torau. Now, fifty years later, that language, called Uruava (also Arawa), has become virtually extinct.

Its former speakers have died out and their offspring have adopted the more prevalent language of their Nasioi-speaking neighbours, a transformation doubtless furthered by marriages between immigrants and earlier residents. Some of Bougainville's languages, both Austronesian and pre-Austronesian, are somewhat mixed, in that they contain certain words and even grammatical features borrowed from neighbouring languages.

Like the Uruava, several other bands of Austronesian-speaking immigrants may have lost both their language and their physical (i.e. genetic) distinctiveness after settling on Bougainville, but those who did not do so (including the Banoni, the Roruana, and the present-day residents of Buka and northernmost Bougainville) remain somewhat lighter in skin colour and generally taller in stature than their non-Austronesian neighbours.

Accompanying the new languages and genes that the Austronesian speakers brought to Buka and Bougainville were several other innovations; these included pottery, obsidian tools, domesticated pigs and chickens, and probably domesticated dogs. It is likely that they also introduced new crops and new techniques of gardening, although the idea of producing food plants - rather than merely collecting or tending wild ones - may have spread to these islands before then.

Moreover, while the languages and the genes of the newcomers remained mostly on Buka and in the coastal areas of Bougainville, the cultural innovation brought in by them diffused throughout the larger island. Thus by the time Europeans 'discovered' Bougainville, all of its inhabitants were growing most of their vegetable food while continuing to collect a few wild-growing ones, such as the starchy pith of the sago palm. While they continued to fish, and to hunt such wild animals as opossums, flying foxes, birds and bats, they also raised pigs and chickens for their occasional feasts, and kept dogs as pets and for assistance in hunting the pigs that had escaped domestication and gone wild. doubtless there were always regional differences in food-getting; fishing figured larger in the lives of coast dwellers than of islanders, and gardening required more effort among mountaineers than among plains-dwellers. but rather than attempt to reconstruct the changes that had taken place in Bougainvillians' cultures from the early days of settlement, let us focus on what they had become just prior to European 'discovery' and colonization.

On evidence that will be given later on this Web site, the number of persons living on Bougainville-Buka just prior to their 'discovery' by Europeans was about 45,000. This number had been reached several centuries earlier and had remained, thereafter, a bout the same. Most of those 45,000 resided in small and widely dispersed hamlets; it was only in a few places (for example, on beaches adjacent to good fishing, on tiny offshore islands) that larger settlements, nucleared villages, were to be found. Except for the island's southeast ti - a heavily forested but otherwise habitable area - the uninhabited, blank, spots on Figure 4 correspond with terrain wholly unsuitable for gardening (e.g. very high mountains or extensive swamps).

Within both hamlets and villages, the basic social unit (for sleeping, for getting, processing, and consuming food; for raising children, etc.) was the family-household. This consisted in some cases of three generations of family members, or of a man and his two, or three, wives and their offspring; but in most cases it consisted of a monogamous couple and their own offspring. In addition, every Bougainvillian became at birth a member of his or her mother's clan, a kind of social unit which had many shapes and many functions (with regard to property rights, choice of spouse, religious practice, etc.).

First of all, those tribes were in most cases very small, consisting of no more than a single village, or a few neighbouring hamlets; in other words, a tribe's 'citizenry' ringed in number from about twenty persons to seldom more than 300. Secondly, the normal relationship between neighbouring tribes was characterized by some degree of hostility, ranging from constant wariness to active warfare. And thirdly, 'chieftainship'- i.e. the kind of leadership characteristic of Bougainville tribes - varied from place to place, with respect to who the leaders were and what they did.

Such were the human condition s on Bougainville and Buka when whites first landed there: in doing so they precipitated, within a few decades, greater changes than had occurred during the previous 28,000 years.

Every adult visitor to Bougainville-Buka these days will know that they contain large quantities of valuable ores, but a first view of the visible landscape is likely to leave two impressions. One is that the topography is monotonously uniform, a jumble of hills and mountains and some flat coastal plains. The other superficial impression is that the soil is everywhere fertile, as indicated by the thick mantle of vegetation that covers all but the two active volcanic peaks.

After a while the initial impression formed of the topography will be confirmed, but even the most unperceptive visitor will learn that the mantle of vegetation is extraordinarily varied, and that the underlying soils also vary greatly in the kinds and amounts of vegetation they can support. while the islands' rich ores last, and are profitably mined, their native residents will probably continue to share, directly or indirectly, in that source of wealth. But when the rich ones are all gone and the two islands' residents have to depend again on what they can grow in their soils, their standards of living will inevitably return to levels simpler than they were when mining began.

Bougainville and Buka Islands form a single land mass separated from one another by a shallow strait 800 metres wide. Together they are about 240 kilometres long, and about 64 kilometres across at their widest point. They are located along a northwest-southeast axis, and are, geologically, part of the Solomon Islands chain. Their total land area is approximately 9000square kilometres, minus some 13 square kilometeres of lakes and some other expanses of freshwater swamp.

About half of the land area is hilly or mountainous, with peaks rising to 1500 to 2400 metres, including several active, dormant, or inactive volcanoes, along with remnants of a geologically ancient plateau of uplifted oral limestone. This coarse-grained classification of natural environment is detailed enough for some purposes, but it is inadequate for anyone seeking deeper understanding of the islands' geographic history and economic prospects. For such purposes scientists have devised a much finer-grained classification composed of 'land units' and 'land systems'.

According to this scheme a land unit is one characterised by 'a particular association of topography, soil, and vegetation' such as, for example, 'a beach with an average slope of about 10 degrees composed of white sand and supporting mixed herbaceous vegetation'; or 'a drainage depression of low gradient composed of submerged peats (up to three feet deep) and supporting tall forest trees chiefly of the *Terminalia brassi* species'.

Needless to say, land systems vary widely in the kinds of human activity they can support. For example, of the two just delineated, the Siwai system can and does support fairly intensive growth of indigenous food plants as well as certain kinds of cash cops; the coastal Jaba system appears to be suitable only for coconuts and plants with similar growing requirements.

There are many other kinds of land systems on these islands that can support no food or cash-crop plants at all - and indeed no other conceivable form of human activity except perhaps swatting mosquitoes or admiring distant views. Some general conditions can be drawn from a map of the islands' forty distinctive land systems. first, the environmental diversity helps partly to explain the cultural diversity that obtains among the islands' several types of subsistence technologies; between coast-dwellers of the north and the east, etc.

While no human society has its way of life determined in all details by its physical environment, none is wholly independent of environmental influences. And for societies with less-developed technologies, including those of the indigenes of Bougainville-Buka, such influences tend to be more decisive.

Second, and more relevant to present-day concerns, a land-systems map reveals, in a way that no amount of guesswork and wishful thinking can deny, how very limited are these islands' surface land resources in terms of economically feasible agriculture.

This needs to be asserted here at the outset, as a caution against the widespread and erroneous impression that in the seemingly verdant soils of Bougainville and Buka, 'anything can be made to grow'. The land 'systems', as just defined, owe their similarities and diversities to several factors, including the islands' geology and climate, and the land-altering activities of its indigenous residents - which, it will be recalled, have been taking place for 28,000 years.

The geological history of these islands has been marked by four land-forming processes; volcanism, coral-limestone growth, tectonic movements, and weathering. At least three p0eriods of major volcanism can be distinguished in the remote past - one prior to the Miocene epoch and two during the Pleistocene. As the fiery cone of Mount Bagana attests, volcanism continues to take place and to alter nearby landscapes.

The growth of coral limestone is also a continuing process along the islands' shores; throughout two large areas - northern Bougainville and Buka, and the Keriaka Plateau - raised limestone constitutes the entire bedrock. Heavy rainfall and year-round tropical temperatures have served to mould all these formations, as well as to build alluvial plains, to cut deep stream beds and to create economically useless swamps. This brings us to the topic of climate.

The climate of the two islands is of the wet-tropical or tropical-rainfall type, and it is remarkably equable the year round. The mean annual temperature at sea level is about 26.7 degrees Centigrade; the monthly sea-level mean temperatures vary only a degree or so above or below that mark, and the average diurnal range at sea level is only about 10.6 degrees.

Temperatures are lower at higher elevations (according to records from comparable places, mean temperature undergoes a drop of 1.35 degrees with every 300 metres), but here also they change within quite narrow monthly and diurnal ranges, and nowhere reach conditions of frost. The alternating wind systems that affect these islands consist of a variable set from the northwest, which occurs between December and April, and a stronger, more continual set from the southeast, which prevails from Mayh to December. These changes in wind have little discernible effedct on (sea-level) temperatures but they exert some influence on patterns of rainfall, particularly in the north.

Average rainfall at sea level is higher in the south (about 3353 millimetres per annum) than in the north (about 2667 millimetres per annum), and regional topographic factors serve to extend these differences somewhat. (Rainfall also tends to increase with elevation, but there are too few records available to indicate how much.) the north-westerly winds (December-April) distribute about the same amount of rainfall over all parts of both islands. during the southeast season (May-December), however, the moisture-laden winds deposit more of their water on the southern slopes of Bougainville's mountains, thereby accounting for the higher average annual rainfall in the south.

As a result of this circumstance, Buka and north Bougainville undergo a dry season during this part of the year. but it is only relatively dry - or rather, relatively less wet; the longest recorded period without rain anywhere in these islands is only sixteen days, and the mean duration of rainless days for both islands is three days or less for all months of the year. The equability of the climate is also indicated by figures for relative humidity. On the basis of observations at sea-level stations, the mean monthly recordings range between only 75 and 86 per cent, and diurnal variations for any one station are even smaller.

Certainly, climate should be considered as one of a number of factors that affect the landscapes of the islands. In addition, of course, climate exercises more direct influences on the lives of the human inhabitants. For example, the unremittingly high temperature and relative humidity undoubtedly affect the health and activities of expatriate visitors from temperate climes. It is reasonable to assume - although difficult to prove - that these climatic factors have some deleterious effects on the indigenes as well, not only in the encouragement they offer to some kinds of diseases but also in their influence upon levels of energy.

To the unsuspecting eye viewing these islands from the air or the sea or even from the ground, humans appear to have made very little impression upon the soils and the profuse vegetation, except for the areas directly affected by mining activities (including the new urban centres and sprawls), and the pockets of expatriate-developed plantations. Even some general awareness of the economic uselessness of many of the land systems cannot entirely erase the visual impression that the indigenous residents have barely begun to exploit the economic potential of their land. The most striking conclusion to be drawn from such a comparison is that in terms of existing types of cultivation and their present ratio of mix, the agricultural potential has already been pushed almost to its limit.

First Contacts with Europeans

The first Europeans known to have sighted either Bougainville or Buka were those aboard the British ship *Swallow*, commanded by Philip Carteret. The Swallow passed within sight of Buka Island on 25 August 1767, but did not approach its sores. Bougainville Island itself was first sighted on 4 July 1768 when the French ships *La Boudeuse* and *L'Etoile* sailed along the eastern coasts of both islands and anchored briefly off Buka. Here is the account of their encounter with the indigenes, written by the expedition's commander, Louis de Bougainville:

> After leaving the passage (west of Choiseul), we discovered to the westward a long hilly coast, the tops of whose mountains were

covered with clouds. ... The 3d in the morning we saw nothing but the new coast, which is of surprising height, and which lies N.W. by W. Its north part then appeared terminated by a point which insensibly grows lower, and forms a remarkable cape.

I have it the name of Cape l'Averdi. On the 3d at noon it bore about twelve leagues W, 1/2 N, and as we observed the sun 's meridian altitude, we were enabled to determine the latitude of this cape with precision. The clouds, which lay on the heights of the land dispersed at sun-setting, and showed us mountain of a prodigious height. On the 4th, when the first rays of the sun appeared, we got sight of some lands to the westward of Cape l'Averdi. It was a new coast (Buka), less elevated than the former, lying N.N.W. Between the S.S.E. point of this land and Cape l'Averdi, there remains a great gap, forming either a passage or a considerable gulf (Buka Passage). At a great distance we saw some hillocks on it. Behind this new coast we perceived a much higher one, lying in the same direction. We stood as near as possible to come near the low lands. At noon we wee about five leagues distant from it, and set its N.N.W. point bearing S.W. by W. In the afternoon three *periaguas* (canoes), in each of which were five or six negroes, came from the shore to view our ships.

They stopped within musket shot, and continued at that distance near an hour, when our repeated invitations at last determined them to come nearer. Some trifles which were thrown to them, fastened on pieces of planks, inspired them with some confidence. They came along-side of the ships, shewing cocoa-nuts, and crying *houca, houca, onelle*!

They repeated these words incessantly, and we afterwards pronounced them as they did, which seemed to give them some pleasure. They did not long keep along-side of the vessel. They made signs that they were going to fetch us cocoa-nuts. We applauded their resolution; but they were hardly gone twenty yards (18 metres), when one of these perfidious fellows let fly an arrow, which happily hit nobody. After that, they fled as fast as they could row; our superior strength set us above punishing them.

These negroes are quite naked; they have curled short hair, and very long ears, which are bored through. Several had dyed their wool red, and had white spots on different parts of the body. It seems they chew betel as their teeth are red. ... This isle, which we named Buka, seems to be extremely well people, if we may judge to by the great number of huts upon it, and by the appearance of cultivation which it has. A fine plain, about the middle of the coast, all over planted with cocoanut trees, another trees, offered a most agreeable prospect, and made me very desirous of finding an anchorage on it; but the contrary wind, and a rapid current, which carried to the N.W. visibly brought us further from it.

During the quarter-century after Bougainville's brief visit, other European vessels sailed within sight of these islands. The first recorded shore visit took place in 1792, when d'Entrecasteaux's vessels lay off the west coast of Buka for a few hours and carried on a lively trade with the indigenes who came to meet them in their canoes. According to one journal of this voyage, the islanders were more eager to obtain red cloth than iron. They are described as astute in bargaining, as well as cheerful and friendly:

> M. de Saint-Aignan played them a fairly lively air on the violin, and the sound of this instrument, new to them, appeared to please them greatly; they laughed and jumped on the benches of their canoes. They offered in exchange for this violin not only the bow which we had already asked of them, but also some clubs they had not yet showed us. (Rossel, *Voyage*, vol. 1. p. 110, quoted in Dunmore 1965, p. 302).

During this period to her European vessels may have made contact with the indigenes of Buka. When Sarah, an English whaler, lay off northern Buka in 1812, the inhabitants traded with the visitors with some degree of familiarity and with apparent appreciation of the utility of the glass bottles and iron they received in exchange for their coconuts and weapons. Thereafter, until the end of the century, Bougainville and Buka were visited by whites for four different purposes: by whalers in search of provisions and fresh crews; by traders in search mainly of coconuts and copra; by labour recruiters; and by explorers, English and German.

Between 1820 and 1860 British, French and American vessels hunted sperm whales in the waters of the northern Solomon Islands, and through them Bougainvillians acquired quantities of weapons, metal tools, cloth and tobacco. During this period some Bougainvillians accompanied the vessels as crew members, sometimes as far as Australia. As a by-product of their contacts, foreign diseases and a liking for liquor were also introduced. Bougainvillians had been trading with other islanders long before Europeans appeared on the scene. Those in the north traded with Nissan and Kilinailau, and those in the south with Shortland, Mono and Fauro.

More is known about the southern trade, in which the Bougainvillean fish and lime (for betelnut chewing). When European traders appeared on the scene, the Bougainvillians began to trade smoke-dried copra in return for steel axe- and adze-blades, machetes and calico. Sometimes a venturesome European trader would cast anchor off the southern Bougainville coast and barter direct with local islanders, but in the beginning most of this trade was carried out through Bougainville Strait islanders acting as middlemen.

Occasionally the latter also acquired live Bougainvillians, by kidnapping or trade, to serve as menials or concubines or for religious sacrifice - and probably for sale to Europeans as labourers. During the 1880s the Strait Islands were under the suzerainty of Gorai, a famous Shortland Island chief, who professed great respect and liking for Europeans. Gorai's influence, though not his actual rule, extended up Bougainville's eastern coast as far as Cape l'Averdy. On one occasion he sent a fleet of his war canoes to the village of Numa Numa, 160 kilometres north of Shortland, and killed a score of its people to avenge the killing of a white trader with whom he was friendly.

A detailed description of a foreign trading visit is provided by the German museum collector, Carl Ribbe, who accompanied a white trader, based on Shortland, on some of his voyages to Bougainville in

1894-5, I reproduce here my translation of an abridged account of one of these visits - this one to the Buin coast just east of Kangu - because of the picture it gave of the manner in which commercial relations between Europeans and indigenes were conducted during that era:

> Mr Tindal and I left Faisi (the main port on Shortland Island) in a small two-masted cutter. ... Around four in the afternoon we drew near to the Bougainville coast ... From where we were the land looked flat in every direction except for two or three 100-metre-high hills directly on the coast (i.e. Kangu Hill). The whole southern Bougainville plain was canopied by tall tress ... and channelled by numerous full-flooded streams. Far to the north-east the horizon was dominated by several high and steep-sided mountains, comprising the Crown Prince Range. ... The narrow strip of hill country between mountains and plain are, like the latter, covered with a high stand of forest but the mountains themselves appeared to be only partly forested. ...
>
> On first seeing these mountains I thought to myself what a rich field of research they must offer to the naturalist. Unfortunately, it would be virtually impossible to get to them, because the country approaching them is said to be densely populated by inhospitable and warlike tribes, whose opposition would prove

even more difficult to overcome because of their ignorance of the power of firearms. Cases have been reported in which such islanders as these have ridiculed their fire-arm bearing opponents, asking what possible effect the latter's noise-making bamboo sticks could have against their own formidable spears and bows and arrows.

it has been my experience that when accompanying a small-sized expedition into the interior of islands in this part of the world, one has less to fear from the hostility of the natives who have already experienced some contact with whites than from those who have never before seen them. Typically, when a small party of explorers is opposed by indigenes with no prior experiences with firearms it is apt to be wiped out in the first assault. Since the thick undergrowth conceals the attackers struck down by bullets, their unwounded fellows remain unaware of the deadliness of firearms and so press their attack fearlessly and relentlessly ...

From where we lay at anchor off shore no houses or canoes were to be seen along the beach, the native villages being located some five to six kilometres inland. ... We remained aboard our cutter that night, then, shortly after sunrise, four of our Shortland Island servants took off for the villages of Suriei and Takerei to inform the villagers that we had come to trade for copra. Each of our messengers was of course armed with rifle and revolver, for we could not rule out the possibility that they might meet up with hostile mountaineers and be obliged to fight. ... Shortly after noon we were hailed from the shore, where we saw many indigenes alongside several piles of copra. The cutter's boat was rowed to the beach to bring back some villagers and their copra, and the trading then began - during which, I should add, we kept our firearms constantly at the ready. . . .

The bartering indigenes were permitted to board the cutter from one side only. While one of us whites occupied himself with the trading, the other kept a close watch to guard against attackhis kind of trading is no great pleasure - indeed, it is long drawn out and boring. However, it is essential not to give up or lose patience; otherwise the blacks would not bother to return to trade another time. The owners of the long strings of dried coconut chunks usually delegate negotiations to one or two of their number, who invariably, in the beginning, demand exorbitant prices.

Then, before any transaction is concluded, each of the villagers o9resent is asked whether he agrees with the terms offered. They appear to have no conception of the monetary value of the various trade items offered to them. It often happens that they will first demand a ridiculously high trade price for their copra, and then in the end be satisfied with a very modest return. Thus, one can obtain 100 coconuts for 65 pfennigs worth of calico, or for 10 coconuts they will accept either a clay pipe worth 1.2/2 pfennigs or 2 sticks of tobacco worth 5. A short muchete costing 40 pfennigs will purchase 50 coconuts, while a long one coasting 1 mark will obtain 100. A box of matches worth 4 pfennigs will obtain 10 coconuts, a Jew's-harp worth 15, 30 coconuts, and an axe worth 1 mark will obtain 100.

From these few examples one can see ... that the indigenes have no idea of the relative values of the trade goods they obtain with their coconuts. The state of affairs, which often results in a disadvantage to the white traders (when indigenes demand too highly priced goods for their coconuts) is the fault of the traders themselves. (How much *more* often, one may inquire, did this 'state of affairs' result in disadvantage to the indigenes?)

The trader has to exercise special care to protect his own interest when the indigenes demand calico for their copra, since the customary method for measuring cloth can work to the latter's advantage. the unit of measure used here is the 'fathom', the span between fingertips of a person's outstretched arms. The length of this span can of course be varied according to the extent that one stretches the arms and the way one holds the cloth.

And it is not surprising that the indigenes insist upon having the measurement done by the man with the longest arms. (One can well understand what diplomacy the trader is called upon to exercise in winning agreement to use a shorter-armed man as a measure.) Distance from outstretched fingertip to nipple also serves as a unit of measure, as does the distance between the outstretched tips of thumb and index finger - these measurements being usd when the indigenes exchange their coconuts, etc. for strings of shell money (*mauu'ai, perasali*).

thus, the whole commerce is a form of barter - which incidentally, is highly profitable to the white traders in this part of the Solomons. The copra, which the trader sells to the schooners that ply these waters, at seven and eight pounds sterling a ton (i.e. 5000 coconuts), he is able to buy from the indigenes at three pounds, thereby realizing a profit of four to five pounds per ton. Among Bougainvillians the trade goods in most demand are hatchers, axes (with metre or half-metre long handles), pocket knives, large blue and red heads for necklaces, small red, blue and white beads used for making ornaments, porcelain bracelets, tobacco and pipes, thin, patterned or red or white calico, plane blades for wood-working, mirrors and Jews' harps.

The indigenes also extend this form of trade among themselves. some goods obtained from the white traders end up in increasingly high prices, so that a distant inlander will pay 300 to 400 coconuts for a hatchet that was obtained at the beach for only 100.

Ribbe went on to say that it was the cop0ra trade that had made the southern Bougainville coast a safer place for outsiders to visit. After about 1870 Bougainvillians were recruited to large numbers for plantations in Queensland, Fiji, Samoa, and New Britain. those of Buka were in especially heavy demand because of their reputation for trustworthiness and industry. for example, the German trader-planner, Richard Parkinson, found his Buka labourers to be invaluable protection from his hostile indigenous neighbours in the Blanche Bay area of New Britain. 'I always licked them fearfully with my Bouka boys of which I have 150.' Some of the Bougainvillians (including Buka) went voluntarily with the European recruiters, evidently eager for the European goods to be earned, or to escape from dangerous situations at home. but others went under duress, as in th case of those kidnapped by the Melbourne vessel *Carl* for work on Fiji.

The *Carl* was owned by an Irish physician, Dr James Murray, who embarked upon his South Seas adventures in 1871 after a series of scandalous scrapes in Australia. After 'recruiting' - that is, kidnapping - nearly eighty indigenes from various islands in the New Hebrides and Solomon Islands and imprisoning them in the vessel's holds, he sailed his ship to northern Bougainville and Buka. Here is Edward Docker's recent reconstruction of what ensued:

> Even King Ghorai of the Shortlands with his mighty war fleet never dared attack Buka, and with visiting ships the big, very black Bukamen paddled out in their twenty-man canoes prepared either to trade or fight as the mood suggested. They never had such a shock in their lives. large lumps of pigiron or cannon slung in ropes crashed down on the canoes, then immediately, as they struggled in the water, with many of them badly gashed and bruised, the boats were among them, hauling them in like tuna. The score was forty the first day, forty-five the next. the earlier captive were now stowed right forward and aft, with the eighty-five Bukamen under the main lurch. Not one was either handcuffed nor leg-ironed.

That evening there was much recrimination on deck among Murray's party about these methods of recruitment - with no attention being paid to what was happening below. Here the Bukamen had broken up their bunks and were using them as implements to force open the hatch. Before long the clamour from the hold drowned out all sounds of the dispute on deck and settled the argument among the white men, at least for the time being. The best-corroborated version of the events of that evening are supplied by a woman, Davescove. He later testified:

'I was awakened about ten by the boy Fallon coming to my bunk, an d asking me for God's sake to come on deck, as the ship was on fire, and they would be all dead men. I went on deck, and to the main hatch, where ai found the passengers and others assembled, called out to the natives to keep quiet. I saw no signs of fire, and went below to the cabin for a minute. While away I heard sounds of firing, and returned on deck, and saw William Scott, Dr Murray, Captain Armstrong, and others firing down into the hold. The natives were fighting amongst themselves, and trying to break open the hatchways, Mount and Morris were firing with revolvers.

'After the natives had been fighting a bit they would stop for a few minutes, and then the firing would cease, and be resumed when the row began again. I went to the cabin after the first row was quieted. I saw Morris there loading a rifle, and Dr Murray loading a revolver. There was firing off and on during the night. I fired myself, once or twice, before I saw Morris and Murray in the cabin. At one o'clock in the morning the mate raised a cry that the natives had charge of the deck, and Dr Murray called out, "Shoot them, shoot them, shoot every one of them."

'When daylight broke, everything was quiet. The shooting continued, off and on, until about three o'clock, or half-past three, when we knocked off altogether. The firing was resumed at intervals of five, ten and fifteen minutes, and sometimes half an hour elapsed between the rows. At four o'clock everything was quiet, and I went into the galley and served out some coffee to the men and passengers. After a bit Dr Murray came aft. Lewis, the second mate, said, "What would people say to my killing twelve niggers before breakfast?" Dr Murray replied, "My word, that's the proper way to pop them off."

'Everything was then quiet, and breakfast was got ready. After breakfast the ladder was put down the hold by the passengers and crew, and the natives were told to come on deck. some of the wounded natives came up; they were wounded in the back, arms, and legs. Those who had a narrow wound were put on one side, and those more dangerously wounded on the other. All the wounded natives who could come up, came up. Two of the good natives were sent down by Dr Murray with ropes, which they fixed round those who were dangerously wounded, so that they could be hauled up. the wounded were separated as I have described by Dr Murray's directions. The passengers were looking on all the time, and Mount and Morris told the natives to do their work.

'I heard them tell them to lay the wounded down, and make fast their hands.

'Dr Murray went forward to the starboard side of the ship, and said, "Well, boys, what do you think of doing with these men?" Mount asked, "What do you think of doing?" "Well," said Murray, "I think that the best we can do is to get the leeward of the island and land them there." A man said, "How far are we from land?" Dr Murray answered, "I don't know, but not very far." Mount said, "You have been gaffer all this time, what are you going to do?" Dr Murray then took four or five of the friendly natives an d went aft, and told them to pick up a man and throw him overboard. There was a boy with six fingers and six toes, who was wounded in the wrist, and he was the first thrown overboard. When Dr Murray told the friendly natives to pick up the boy, the other natives screamed "No, no, no!" He was lifted onto the rail, and Dr Murray pushed him overboard. He was the first who was thrown overboard. At this, all the Bougainville men who could do so, jumped overboard.'

In the end the total of natives killed outright or tossed badly wounded into the sea amounted to seventy. Another fifteen or so of the unwounded may have swam safely ashore, which now left on board the seventy-six so-called 'friendly' natives. One result of the abortive mutiny was that the Malaitamen had completely abandoned their former overhasty ideas of escape.

Some of the Europeans who took part in these outrages were eventually arrested and sentenced to death or terms in prison, but the agile and ingratiating Dr Murray tuned Queen's evidence and escaped punishment altogether.

The most detailed account of labour recruiting on Bougainville - Buka is that of Douglas Rannie, who accompanied a recruiting expedition on board an Australian vessel as government agent. The vessel stopped twice off Bougainville-Buka in search of recruits for the Queensland sugar fields; first at an unspecified point off Bougainville's northwest coast, and then off Buka. The different receptions accorded the vessel at these two points serve to show how different the inhabitants of the two islands had by then become in terms of their experience and sophistication in dealing with whites:

> On the morning of the 25th of June we lowered our boats about eight o'clock and made towards the shore. This being the weather side, a very heavy surf was breaking on the beach; so heavy, indeed, that for some time we thought we should have to give up all idea of getting into communication with the natives, whom we saw in large numbers lined up on the sand.
>
> There appeared to be two tribes assembled. They did not seem to be upon amicable terms, as they held aloof from one another. They were all heavily armed with very long bows and sheaves of arrows. Besides these weapons some carried spears, and each man had suspended from his shoulder a tomahawk, club, or heavy wooden sword. The tribes were distinguished by the colour of their head-dress. This was composed of a hat exactly resembling an egg-shaped lamp-globe and of similar size. These hats were made of basket-work, and beautifully covered and

sewn with the skin of the pandanus leaf. They reminded me more than anything else of the baskets used in billiard-rooms for pool and pyramid balls. The opening was not much wider, although it might have admitted a cricket ball; into this the natives towed their long, woolly hair. The large amount of hair they managed to stuff in caused the hats to stick up jauntily on the side of the head. The hats worn by one tribe were all white, while those worn by the other were stained a bright red.

Pulling along the coast we came to a smooth part, and were able to approach nearer the islanders. After a lot of persuasion we induced them to approach nearer to each other as well as to us. Both tribes wished to enter into communication with us, and both had stuff for barter. As neither would entirely trust the other, they each left a strong armed p0arty immediately behind them in the scrub as guards. The mate, with his boat stern first, cautiously approached what seemed to be the most moderate break in the surf, and I directed his attention to the heavy break which occurred with every third or fourth wave outside the ordinary surf. As a man came out neck-deep in the water, holding a young sucking pig over this had, the mate ventured too much. A huge wave broke over the bows of his boat, filled her and swept here right up on the beach. The boat's crew leaped out before she grounded, having first secured their rifles. Many of the islanders ran for their weapons, but others professed to offer assistance. In the meantime we were outside the influence of the surf, and covered the other boat's crew with our rifles. The natives ashore seemed to be of two minds. Some, I thought, desired to assist our men, while others were inclined to go for loot. but the fact that our men still retained their arms ashore, and we were almost out of range of their arrows, and had them well covered, decided them to help us in our difficulty and trust to our generosity for remuneration. A number of them turned to with a will, and after the mate had given them all the print and calicoes, besides beads, pipes, and tobacco, which he had in the trade box (the axes, tomahawks, long knives, and butcher's knives were in the bottom of the boat), they re-launched the boat. but alas! before the boat's crew could get her under way with their oars, a great rolling sea caused her to broach-to and capsize, and surge in towards the beach, bottom up, with the crew underneath. One by one they struggled out. The mate was dragged out with a horrible gash on the back of his head and neck, from which the blood flowed freely. Hastily we unbent the painter and the sheet of our big-sail, and backing the boat in as far as we deemed safe through the surf, we threw the boat's crew the rope. They made it first to the mate, and we were able to draw him through the surf to us. Pulling out to a safe distance beyond the breakers, we rendered what first aid we could to the wounded man.

A terrible scene ensued ashore. The natives of both tribes rushed down to the boat, dragged her up on to the beach, and fought savagely for the axes, tomahawks, and knives that were lying in from two to three feet (60 to 90 centimetres) of water. Two natives would be struggling for an axe. One would manage to free his arm, with the axe aloft' and the next instant it would be brought crash, down through the skull of the other unfortunate one. Several could be seen fighting and slashing each other with the long knives and butcher knives, as they rolled over and over each other in the water. Those ashore along the fringe of scrub took up the fight, and a general battle ensued. The arrows were flying in the air like showers of hail. Presently a large body of men charged out from the scrub, on those nearest the boat (they had manoeuvred round through the back of the scrub from the tribe of the white hats), and making a wild dash among the bowmen of the red hats, mowed them down with tomahawks and hardwood swords before the red hats had time to unsling their weapons. The red hats then took to flight, but were followed by the white hats with showers of arrows until the bush gave them shelter.

There must have been upwards of a thousand engaged in the fray, and the casualties were very numerous. Seeing that we could not do much more until our second boat was patched up, we made for the north end of Bougainville and came to anchor at Buka Island.

We were visited at Buka Island by large numbers of islanders in many canoes. The canoes carried from ten to sixty men in each. As many of them were as high in the sides as our own little vessel, we made a rule that canoes were to be allowed on one side only, and that the starboard. The port side was to be kept clear, as well as the main deck on the port side; so the ship was roped off fore and aft amidships. We had also to be constantly on the watch and always armed; for, on the slightest show of carelessness on our part, or of being off guard, we should all have been massacred for the sake of loot.

One of our boatmen told me that on a previous visit he had been shown on a clear day the hull and masts of a vessel lying on the horizon in deep water. She had been taken and looted by the natives and then sunk. We secured the services of an islander here as an interpreter. He was the only one able to speak English. He told us that his name was 'Maggy', and that he had worked for a Mr Farrell in Samoa. Maggy piloted us to quite a number of villages, but found no one anxious to emigrate to Queensland. The villages were kept as clean and ship-shape as any in the Shortlands, and the natives displayed as much taste in the manner in which their plots of flowers and flowering plants about their houses were attended to. As the Shortlands I noticed that the dead were buried in the ground and large cairns of stones were piled over the graves, these again were filled in with soil, and the interstices planted with bright and fragrant flowers. but here the dead were disposed of in quite a different manner.

We had an opportunity while on a visit to one of the villages of seeing their strange funeral ceremony. The corpse was carried down to and over the ref by a few of the deceased's comrades, followed by a crowd of women wailing and performing strange antics. At the edge of the reef the remains were placed in a canoe, paddled out some hundred yards or so, and with a few heavy stones attached were sunk to the bottom. although five from any particular amount of general sickness, and physically as fine a race of people as we had so far met, 80 per cent of them seemed to be afflicted with a disagreeable skin disease they called 'buckwah' (?).

This disease breaks out in patches on the body in the form of a number of small dry rings, resembling ringworm. They spread till the whole body becomes covered with a mass of dry, scaly rings, which comes off a flakes and dust. I have cured many of the sufferers with a mixture of sulphur and kerosene, applied with a large paint brush. Clean-skinned natives seem to have a horror of contracting the disease.

We found the islanders very skilful in the manufacture of spears and arrows, and many of their weapons were tastefully inlaid with mother-of-pearl. Pearl-shell appears to be fairly plentiful in those regions. From the many patches of reefs we sailed over. I believe large quantities of shell could be obtained. Three days were spent in visiting villages scattered here and there, but all our recruiter's eloquence could not induce any of the natives to engage in the Queensland sugar industry. So the skipper decided to make a move the following day. That evening two large canoes came along from some foraging expedition. Their crews, numbering about forty each, were quite jubilant over some foray, or success. They clicked their paddles on the side of their canoes, keeping time to a wild chant or war song.

The paddles of these canoes had each the design of a dancing demon stained on it in permanent black and red dyes. Crouched despondent in the bottom of one of the two canoes, we noticed, as they came alongside, a wild, powerful-looking man. After an animated conference with the savages in the canoes, our interpreter Maggy approached the skipper and me, and told us that the savages had a captive in one of their canoes whom they wished to dispose of by selling them to us. I said that the strict meaning of the Act would not allow any such mode of recruiting. Yet as the circumstances of the case seemed very peculiar, I determined that I would go into them very carefully.

Impressing upon Maggy that he must speak the truth, and nothing but the truth, I elicited through him from the canoe savages that the man whom they now wanted us to take was a captive they had made upon their present expedition. They were taking him home with them, there to be dealt with in a way that even Maggy hesitated to describe. I inferred that he was to be put to death, and eaten. I got Maggy to explain to the captive that if he chose to come of his own free will on board of us he could do so, and that if he chose to leave the ship at any place to the islands no one would prevent him. As he came on board under peculiar circumstances, the same circumstances would allow him to go ashore anywhere he liked where the ship should touch before leaving for Queensland. As we had an interpreter on board who could speak his own language, the whole of the nature of the work expected of South Sea Islanders on Queensland plantations would now be fully explained to him, together with the nature and terms of agreement. but that he would not be called upon to enter into that agreement until some time during the trip when others might be signed on.

All this I was confident Maggy faithfully explained to him, and he came very joyfully aboard. In return, the savages, at their captive's hands, received a bundle of fancy-coloured print, in which were rolled up some glass beads, paint, tobacco, a couple of butcher's knives, and a tomahawk. I made the parcel of trade come from the captive as a ransom paid by himself, and not as the price paid for a slave. Thus we got our first recruit, and he was entered on the Passenger List as No. 1, Cheeks and Buka, Bougainville. He was about twenty-five years of age, well built and muscular-looking, with a huge head of hair hanging in a mass of ringlets down to his shoulders. Each ringlet was plastered thick with lime and cocoa-nut. We soon set one of the crew to work with the scissors and his locks were consigned to the deep. Cheeks was quite pleased with the change, and was anxious to adopt European habits at once, so great was his delight at escaping from his enemies. And yet, he told me afterwards, he had never seen a white man in his life before.

The effects of these early encounters between Bougainvillians and white must have varied widely. some of the former, mainly coast-dwellers, and especially those of Buka and northern Bougainville, became well acquainted with the material goods and customs of whites, and with their characters, both good and bad. Many, however, experienced nothing of the new alien influences except the occasional steel tool that filtered to them through coastal intermediaries. One of the most detailed accounts of that period was written by H.B. guppy, the naval surgeon attached to a British exploring expedition to the Solomon Islands in 1882.

This writer tarried for several months in the islands of the Bougainville Strait and made several visits to the south coast of Bougainville itself. guppy collected much useful information concerning the indigenes and the natural resources of southern and eastern Bougainville, including specimens of ore that led him to make the prophetic statements: 'A sample of stream tin from the southeast part of Bougainville was given to me by the Shortland chief. Copper will not improbably be found in association with the serpentine rocks of these islands.'

Until 1884 Bougainville-Buka continued to remain outside the administrative domain of any European power, although British subjects (including some Australians) were most in evidence there, as visiting traders and labour recruiters. This situation began to change in 1834 when Germany annexed northeast New guinea (Kaiser-Wilhelmsland) and the Bismarck Archipelago. This action moved Queensland, and eventually Britain, to annex Papua (i.e., southeast New Guinea). Bougainville and Buka were not officially added to the German colony until 1899, but by an exchange of notes with Britain, in 1886, these islands (along with Shortland, Choiseul, and Isabel) were declared to be within the German sphere of influence. In fact, German influence began to extend to Bougainville and Buka some years earlier in the persons of traders, explorers and recruiters of labourers for plantations on Samoa, the Bismarck Archipelago and elsewhere.

The best-known of those early Germans was the Richard Parkinson referred to earlier. Parkinson had moved to New Britain from Samoa in 1882. (His wife was sister to the much-married Emma Forsyth - 'Queen Emma' - who had gone from Samoa to New Britain earlier and had established extensive trading and plantation enterprises in the

Duke of York Islands and on Blanche Bay.) Froi his New Britain base Parkinson made many trips to Bougainville and Buka, trading, recruiting, and collecting natural history specimens; he recorded his observation in several scientific papers and in his lengthy book: *Dressig Jahre in der Sudsee* (Thirty Years in the south Seas.) In summarizing his findings, Parkinson reported that by the turn of the century the coastal inhabitants had become fairly familiar with Europeans, through trading with them or serving on their plantations on New Britain and elsewhere, but that the interior of the larger island remained 'virtually closed-off'.

Ignorance about Bougainville's inland areas during that era can be attributed partly too its physical inaccessibility, partly to their inhabitants' ways of life, and partly to the behaviour of the white visitors themselves. During the nineteenth century, and probably for centuries and millennia before, the native people were separated into numerous minute tribes whose interrelations, if any, were typically hostile, with the exception of occasional instances of intertribal trade.

Moreover, this normal state of hostility was more often than not intensified in specific cases where one tribe was made up of coast-dwellers and the other of islanders. This antagonism was for a time reinforced by the appearance on the scene of white traders and labour against their traditional enemies. for some islanders the only way to acquire the eagerly sought European trade goods was by raids against coastal settlements. Also it is likely that many of the inlanders who ended up in the hands of labour recruiters arrived there through kidnapping by coastal middlemen.

In addition, much of the initial hostility shown to whites was the direct result of the latters' bahaviour. for every Parkinson visiting these shores - for every white who viewed the indigenes with intellectual curiosity and treated them with some degree of fairness and humanity - there were many others who considered them to be subhuman and handled them fraudulently and brutally. before some measure of colonial authority was established, the only constraint exercised by most traders and recruiters was their wish again to trade and recruit there some day. Here is Parkinson's description of the labour recruiters' part in this contact:

> The recruiters concentrated their efforts on the filling of their ships. From place to place they went, searching the coast up and down with their boats, and, whether or not, came into conflict with the natives who could not make themselves understood, and who knew from experience and hearsay the methods of recruiting labourers which they regarded as pure kidnapping.

No wonder, then, that the Bougainvillians of that era earned reputations for hostility against whites, all whites. As Parkinson recorded:

> Murders of white men were recorded every year, murders that were brought about by the victims' own fault, or, as was unfortunately the case, done to avenge the misdeeds of other recruiters. Every white person was regarded as an enemy, recruiter, trader or missionary; the crime of another has often caused the death of a perfectly harmless and peaceful man.

In 1902 the Catholic Society of Mary extended its missionary endeavours in the Solomon Islands by setting up a station on Bougainville's eastern coast, near Kieta. Then, in 1905 the German colonial administration at Rabaul established a post at Kieta, and at about the same time a few European planters and traders began to settle along the eastern and northern coasts of Bougainville and along Buka's western and southern coasts. Between 1899 (when these islands were officially annexed) and 1905, German political control - such as it was - was administered by means of occasional visits of officials from Rabaul

The German Era

German merchants and shipping firms began to move into the Pacific in the 1850s, intent upon building up a trade empire to equal or surpass Britain's. their first south Seas base was established at Apia, Samoa, in 1856. Within a few years they had extended their trading activities, including shore-based stores, to the Marshalls, the Gilberts (Kiribati), the Ellice (Tuvalu), Tonga and Fiji. About 1870 their agents became the first traders to brave the frontier hardships of New Britain, thereby becoming the forerunners of German sovereignty there.

For a number of years after that the Germans' commercial operations were carried on without government backing' even the unification of Germany did not immediately change that, Bismarck having been initially opposed to colonials. In time, however, German merchants and patriots had their way, and the government adopted a policy in favour of empire and world-girdling naval powers, in deliberate competition with Britain.

The first product of this policy change in the south Sea was in the form of even stronger support for German firms in New guinea. In 1884 this led to annexation of northeast New gui8nea (Kaiser-Wilhemsland) and the Bismarck Archipelago - which, as noted earlier, prompted Britain's annexation of Papua. For a number of years thereafter the German government left it to the *Newguinea-Kompagnie*, the new colony's largest plantation and trading firm, to govern it. this arrangement worked more or less successfully (i.e., profitably) for a few years, mainly because of profits from tobacco-growing around New guinea's Astrolabe Bay. However, the company's losses elsewhere in the colony, plus the coast of trying to govern, forced it to turn administration over to the government in 1899, the year in which the colony's boundaries were extended to include Bougainville and Buka. After that, occasional visits were made to the latter by German officials but a permanent government station was not established there (at Kieta) until 1905.

Official German policy valued the colony principally as a source of raw materials and as a strategic outpost in Germany's expanding commercial and political empire. Insofar as the area's indigenous peoples figured in these objectives, they were looked upon mainly as private producers of raw materials, as labourers in European enterprises, as consumers of European manufactures, and a accessories of this official policy it should be added that it was not indifferent to the indigenes' 'welfare'; it merely reflected the widespread European view of that era, that the best thing one could do for 'primitives' everywhere was to inculcate in them *waitman's* habits of work, thrift, civic orderliness, sexual morality, hygiene, religion, etc. Some whites in the colony dealt with the indigenes as if they were less than human and hence to be exploited like domesticated animals, but official policy was more positive and humane, especially under the aegis of Dr Albert Hahl, whose tenure of governorship lasted from 1896 to 1914.

From 1899 to 1914 the principal commercial activity on Bougainville and Buka was growing coconuts for export. by 1914 nearly 30,000 hectares of land on Bougainville-Buka had been alienated by whites, principally for coconut plantations. this represented only 3.3 per event of the islands' total land area, but some 10 per cent of all the areas suitable for growing coconuts, and a much larger proportion of such land favourably situated for commercially feasible production. The manual labour used on copra production was supplied mainly by the two islands' own indigenes.

(Some efforts were made to employ Asians for such work, but this source proved in time to be too expensive and unreliable.) In addition, many of these islands' indigenes were employed to work on plantations elsewhere in the Pacific, especially in Samoa and, for r a while, in the British Solomon Islands. Some plantations were able to obtain some or all of their labour from nearby villages, either on a contract or non-contract basis, but all 'overseas' labour, that is all individuals having to be transported by boat from home area to place of individuals having to be transported under contract and was subject to Administration supervision.

The usual term of contract was three years and the legal minimum wage was five marks a month plus keep. (At that time a mark was roughly equal to a shilling.) Most employment were officially licensed to punish their labourers physically, usually by flogging, for breaches of discipline, and when runaways were caught they were forcibly returned to work, if necessary by armed police. On the other hand the Administration attempted to see to it that such labourers were fed, housed and doctored well enough to keep them active and reasonably healthy, and their employers were required to repatriate them at the end of their contracts.

The Administration attempted to ensure that any individual entering into a labour contract did so voluntarily. However, the methods whereby unsophisticated indigens were usually recruited - by inducements that never materialized, or in terms that they did not comprehend - rendered this measure meaningless. for many indigenes the first inkling of what a contract meant occurred only when they found themselves forcibly detaianed at work in places without native women and far from home.

Contemporary apologists for this indenture system asserted that forced disciplined labour of this kind was a civilizing influence, the best way to transform barbarous and inherently lazy natives into useful and presumably happier members of the wider colonial society. It was even held that such work was essential to save them from the mental and physical stagnation that allegedly resulted when the stimulus of intertribal warfare was denied them. (As we shall see, the white stereotyped that 'natives' are 'lazy', like those concerning their sexual morals, and religious beliefs, is both ancient and durable.)

As for other effects of working and living on a white-owned plantation, it is questionable how much civilization rubbed off onto men who were herded together in barracks and work gangs, and consigned to such ranks as bush clearing and coconut splitting.

The long-term absence of a labourer also affected his home community. Most indigenous communities of Bougainville-Buka were so small and closely knit that the absence of several of their productive male members left them economically and socially upset; households were left without male food producers, and families without husbands and fathers. In some instances the proportion of absent males was so large and birth rates fell so sharply that the authorities attempted to limit recruiting, through as much from concern for future labour supply as for the welfare of the communities themselves.

Some plantations were able to draw much of their labour from neighbouring settlements, with or without contract. From the indigenes; point of view, this arrangement was far better, the labourers were able to earn some cash income without giving up their familiar satisfactions, and their communities were able to maintain a more normal way of life.

Although a large proportion of the colony's copra exports was produced by the indigenes in their own small groves, the German authorities were concerned mainly with the white-owned plantations. Very little was done to transform the indigenes into successful independent producers, or to stimulate other forms of indigenous economic enterprise. Instead the German authorities sought to civilize their charges by organizing them into an administrative hierarchy, and by requiring them to pay a head tax and to work without compensation on public projects.

As soon as any indigenous community was brought under 'control', i.e., as soon as it was made reasonably safe for whites to visit it to trade or recruit labour, one of its residents was appointed to the office of *luluai* (the word for chief in one of th4 languages of New Britain).

The German official in charge usually made an effort to appoint the community's established leader, or at least one of its more respected elders, but often the office was given to the most ingratiating man. (In many instances a community's real leader shoe not to occupy this office and put forward a nonentity instead.)

The duties given to a *luluai* were varied: collection of the annul head tax, supervision and government recruiters, arbitration of minor local disputes, etc. Instead of a salary, such officials received 10 per cent of the tax money collected by them, and they were given badges of office in the form of a bat and a silver-beaded stick.

To assist the *luluai* there was also appointed an interpreter (*tultul*), and a medical orderly (*doctorboy*). The former was a man with some fluency in Pidgin, usually an ex-plantation labourer. The latter's job was to dispense bandages and simple medicines and to enforce elementary sanitation measures. Under German administration all physically fit indigenous males past childhood were required to contribute unpaid work on public projects for up to four weeks a year. such projects included road-building and a maintenance, and work on government plantations and stations.

In addition, forced labour of this kind was used as a means of punishing fractious individuals and, more generally, as a device for inculcating indigenes with the civilized value of sustained physical work on behalf of 'public welfare'. The public welfare in question was, of course, chiefly that the colonial authorities and businesses.

The system of taxation introduced by the German authorities was regarded by them more as a civilizing device than a source of revenue. When an area was first brought under administrative control it became subject to taxation, but on a graduated scale. In highly colonized areas, like the area around Rabaul, where the indigenes had many opportunities to earn money, the tax rate was ten marks a year. Elsewhere it was seven, or five, marks a year, according to the area's state of commercial development.

Where taxation applied, every physically fit male over about twelve years of age was assessed, except for a white for at least ten months during the current tax year. for those taxable individuals unable to pay, the alternative was work on a public project for about fourteen extra days a year. Whether or not this taxation helped to civilize the indigenes, it undoubtedly contributed to the economic progress of the colony, both by encouraging work on white-owned enterprises and in the production by indigenes of cash-earning crops. It is doubtful, however, that it served to educate those taxed in the virtuous necessity of taxation as a duty of responsible citizenship.

As for other measures of education, the German authorities left formal schooling, such as it was, almost entirely in mission hands. What effects did these colony-wide policies and practices have on Bougainville-Buka? By 1914, large numbers of Bougainvillians were employed on plantation s, both locally and in the Bismarck Archipelago. They were generally known as 'Buka boys', and easily identified as such by their darker skin colour'; they had become favourably known for their industrious ness and what seemed to be eagerness to learn new skills. but exactly how many were so engaged and that proportion of them worked away from home is not recorded.

What is certain, however, is that these two islands were only partially under the Administration's control. Bika, being smaller, less mountainous, and nearer to Rabaul, was better explored and subjugated, as was the northern end of Bougainville and the coastal areas immediately north and south of Kieta. the rest of the larger island was uncontrolled, the Greater Buin Plain - where the usual state of intertribal warfare was further complicated by the illegal recruiting of labourers for plantations in the British Solomon Islands.

At one point it was proposed to set up a government station on the Buin coast to assist 'in pacifying the tribes, who even at the present time have pitched battles, and render accessible to (legal) recruiting this virile stamp of men. Occasional (official) tours and punitive expeditions cannot cr4eate quietude in these regions. (From the official *Report on New Guinea*, quoted in Rowley 1958, p..5)

The first whites to establish permanent residence on Bougainville-Buka were Marist missionaries, who founded a station at Kieta in 1902. Three years previously the mission had set up headquarters on Shrotland Island, and prior to the move to Kieta had begun to win Bougainvillian converts in the person of the many young people who became workers and trainees at the Shortland station. (Then and previously, it will be recalled, there was frequent contact between Shortland Islanders and the Buin-speaking peoples of southeast Bougainville. Many of the latter lived on Shortland in a stage of benign semi-bondage or of concubinage.)

The German authorities encouraged the Marists to extend their influence on Bougainville-Buka itself - including the acquisition of land - but more with a view to economic development than to evangelization.

By 1906 relations between whites and coast-dwelling Bougianvillians had reached a state of peaceable interaction. Here are some extracts from an account by Parkinson, who, it will be recalled, was the German planter based in Rabaul who made frequent visits to these islands trading and recruiting labourers for New Britain plantations. this account, which is translated freely, is in the form of a travelogue describing the coasts of the larger island.

Only those parts dealing with the inhabited strips of the coasts are included here. It may be safely concluded that the remaining coastal areas contained no indigenous settlements of any size, except those along the southwest coast which Parkinson did not include in his circuit. Travelling north from Bougainville's southeast point, Cape Friendship, he first mentions indigenes in his description of the mouth of the Luluai River, where he records the presence of:

> small canoes drawn up along the banks, which indicate the proximity of indigenes - a conclusion that is borne out by the sight of some native gardens along both banks of the river ...

> At the mouth of the Luluai there are usually many indigenes to be seen, and although they are invariably armed with their bows and barbed arrows they are not as dangerous as they seem. they came to this spot to fish, their actual settlements being north of here in the Kaianu district. ...

> North of the Lulua the steep and deeply fissured foothills of the Crown Prince Range reach almost to the coast, and in Kaianu they terminate abruptly at the coast itself. the palm-shaded houses of

the villages in this area are built on the hillside slopes, and far inland the sight of forest clearings and rising columns of smoke indicates the presence of native gardens. ...

North of Kaianu is the district of Koromira whose coastal area is well populated. According to reports, inland Koromira is also well people, and by indigenes who are described by the coast dwellers as being so warlike that the latter must keep themselves continuously armed. (This is the characteristic way that coast dwellers describe their inland neighbours in this part of the world.) ...

Proceeding north along the coast we came to the village of Toboroi whose inhabitants are a peaceful folk who came originally from Shortland Island. during the period when the great Shortland chief, Gorai, was extending his rule over much of south Bougainville, the Toboroi people constituted his northern-most outpost. ...

Next comes the Toboroi roman Catholic Mission which was established in 1902 (the first permanent European settlement on the island), and after that Kieta, where a police station has recently been set up by the German administration.

Further along, in Arawa Bay, one is treated to a sight which is becoming increasingly rare in the South Seas. From time to time the mountaineers who live inland from Arawa come down to the coast, either to fish or to view with wonder the sight of a European vessel. they come in throngs, of both sexes and all ages, mainly for mutual protection but perhaps also because it would be unsafe to leave anyone behind if the men alone were to come (since no village is able to trust its neighbours). They arrive completely naked, their black bodies painted red or white, and carrying their bows and arrows and spears. these wild-looking bands rush at the visitors with loud cries, but they turn out to be quite harmless. Their shouts and gesticulations are simply their way of expressing excitement and astonishment at the unfamiliar sight of whites.

Everything we possessed excited their amazement and wonder, whether it be a piece of coloured calico, a height-hued bead, a mirror, a knife, an axe, a fishhook, or whatever. They readily exchange their finely wrought weapons for cheap trinkets, behaving like children who have just en given a long-wanted toy. In due course even the females overcome their initial shyness and crowd around us to clamour for their share of the beautiful new things. Speaking of the women, while many of the young girls are favoured with strong slender bodies and pleasant faces and ivory white teeth, the older ones, with their wrinkled skin and deeply furrowed faces, look like nothing so much as Blocksberg witches. . . .

In recent years it has been possible to recruit some of these mountaineer males to work on plantations in the Bismarck Archipelago. After they have served out their indentures and returned home they will probably, through their example, influence a large number of their fellows to engage in works away from home. . . .

Continuing north along the coast some fourteen kilometres past Cape Mabiri, one comes to the village of Bagovegove which is located in what evidently is a very vulnerable position. When I first visited this village in 1886 it had just been rebuilt after having been destroyed by hostile mountain-dwellers. In 1889 it it was again wiped out by the latter, to be rebuilt in 1894, and again burnt to the ground by the same enemies in 1895. However, since its last reconstruction in 1898, it has survived unscathed, mainly because of its reinforcement by immigrants from north Bougainville and east Buka.

On my visit to Bagovegove in 1902 I counted eighteen large war canoes and over fifty ordinary ones, which bore witness to a large population and was confirmed by the sight of swarms of men, women and children around the houses built along the beach. In 1889 I also spotted a small village, Sapiu, about one kilometre south of Bagovegove, but this was subsequently destroyed by the mountain people and evidently not rebuilt. . . .

Inland from Bagovegove and Sapiu and south of the latter is an extensive area of swampy terrain, and the inlanders who live on the higher ground around it are described by the coastal peoples as being fierce and unrelenting cannibals, ever eager to capture victims either by open attack or ambush. Now whether it is the inlanders who are the real aggressors, or the coastal dwellers themselves, I am not able to prove.

I am however inclined to the belief that it is the latter who are the original aggressors, in their eagerness for bloodletting and booty, and that the actions of the inlanders are nothing other than reprisals. . . .

the inhabitants of the strip of coast, known as the Numanuma area, have on occasion been hostile to whites as well as to their inland neighbours. In the 1870s, for example, the small trading steamer Ripple was attacked here by the local people; its captain, a Mr Ferguson, was murdered, along with several of his crew. Although the handful of surviving crew members were badly wounded, they managed to pull up anchor and escape. 'Revenge was not long in coming.

It happened that Captain Ferguson enjoyed the friendship of the Shortland chief, Gorai, and the latter sent a fleet of warriors who wiped out Numanuma and its inhabitants during a month long campaign. Since that time the indigenes hereabouts have remained more or less peaceful (toward Whites), but they continue to bear the reputation of being the most untrustworthy people in Bougainville. . . .

Between Numanuma and Point Nehus (now the site of Inus plantation) are many small inlets and flat stretches of beach which are ideally suited to native settlement. Indeed, before 1888 there were numerous settlements just here, but now the only remains of them consist of their coconut palms. . . .

Just north of Point Nehus the mountains rise abruptly behind the narrow coastal plain and form the site for many native settlements, their well-built houses, laid out in rows, being clearly visible from the coast. continuing north towards Cape l'Averdy, the coastal plain broadens and the foothills become less steep. In the waters off these shores one almost always sees canoes, engaged either in fishing or in trade expeditions to nearby settlements. . . .

Off Bougainville's northeast cape lies the inhabited island of Teop, but on the mainland opposite Teop one has to go a considerable distance inland before reaching any settlements, on account of the continual state of warfare between Teop and the inlanders. the latt4er are industrious gardeners; on occasion they bring large quantities of produce, mainly taro, down to the beach to trade. In addition they are also very warlike and are rarely to be seen unarmed.

On the various occasions when I have visited them in them in their mountain village, I have invariably found them to be friendly and hospitable, but such relation do not obtain between people of separate village. In every settlement I have visited unexpectedly he must not consider it to be a sign of hostility to him if he finds himself suddenly confronted with a crowd of men threatening him with their weapons; for, as soon as he is recognized, his hosts' hostility will immediately give way to joyous greetings.

Future exploring expeditions to this region need fear no great difficulties from the local indigenes, provided that their leaders exercise tact and maintain calm. However, a high-handed attitude on the part of the visitors, or an unjust action or display of violence, will quickly have the effect of turning friendship into hostility, and will force the expedition to turn back. . . .

The harbour of Cape l'Averdy could become an excellent base for opening up the nearby countryside, which contains large areas suitable for cultivation and which could be developed without damage to the interests of the indigenes. In fact, in my opinion there are many places on Bougainville where the local indigenes would welcome the establishment of plantations, in which their own labour would be involved. for not only would this kind of development contribute to more peaceful relations among the different tribes in the areas in question, but it would provide markets for the indigenes' own garden produce. . . .

Some four kilometres west of the harbour at Cape l'Averby lies the small harbour and village of Tinputz. Then, for the next twelve kilometres or so up to Laua Harbvour, the coast itself is uninhabited, the nearest settlements being a long way inland. Within this uninhabited stretch of coastland are many thousands of hectares of excellent agricultural land, the best in all northern Bougainville. here also are several fine harbours, numerous year-round streams, good soil, regular rainfall - and no indigenous settlements to be disturbed by the establishment of plantations.

Moreover, the area further inland and the nearby districts contain a sizeable population already accustomed to sending young men away to work . . . . West of Bantu Bay the coastline becomes high and steep, but here and there are to be seen shallow little bays bordered by sandy beaches which provide sites for a number of indigenous settlements. Here along the coast one frequently meets fleets of twenty and thirty canoes, each one containing twenty to thirty people, there being a lively trade between here and Buka.

In addition to the beach villages found along this stretch of coast there are a number of others located along the top of the seaside cliffs. In fact, for a number of years this area has been a major source of plantation labour; the local people are less timid of whites than their fellow islanders elsewhere, and it is possible to communicate with them in Pidgin English. . . .

Continuing westward through Buka Passage and south of the island of Sohano we enter a very large bay, bordered on the east by the Sailo Peninsula and protected on the west by the Taiof and a number of other smaller islands. Here we are visited by indigenes whom we have met before, on the other side of the peninsula. this time, however, they are travelling not in their large war- or sea-going craft, but in small outrigger canoes, or even on roughly constructed rafts. the have crossed the narrow peninsula to fish in these relatively calm water, and evidently find the canoes and rafts better suited to this activity than their larger craft. the whole of the peninsula is given over to cultivation, mostly of taro and banana. . . .

Southward along Bougainville's west coast one passes the foothills of the mighty Emperor Range, and in some of the coastal valleys of the foothills are to be seen small garden clearings. The mountains hereabouts are said gto be well populated, but the inhabitants are reputed to be hostile to all outsiders. . . .

Further along one enters broad Empress Augusta Bay, which acquired an evil reputation during the era of uncontrolled labour recruiting for the plantations of Australia and Fiji. Time after time recruiting vessels were attacked by the local indigenes and all their people killed. Since that era, however, the situation here has greatly changed. the coastal villages, now largely depopulated through emigration, are threatened by the inland mountaineers. ?

Scarcely a quarter of the inhabitants of this once thickly populated coastal area now remain, and some whole villages have entirely disappeared. 'And what used to be a dangerously unfriendly populace has become far less so; in my frequent visits to the surviving villages I invariably meet with a hospitable reception. These villages are regularly visited by traders from Shortland Island, and for the past few years no whites have been attacked.

Turning now to the island of Buka, it is quite densely populated, and for this reason alone does not provide much opportunity for the establishment of European plantations. the indigenes of Buka belong to the same race as those of Bougainville, and have for many years been offering their services as labourers. . . .

Except fort the labour, however, neither Bougainville nor Buka has much to offer in the way of local produc4ts; and such produce as there is is usually acquired as a sideline by recruiting vessels. With respect to these island, but commerce in that area is largely in the hands of English traders based on Shortland Island, and is thus of little value to us Germans.

By 1914 additional Marist mission stations had been established at Patapatuai (Buin), Koromira, Torokina, and Burunotui (Buka); and the headquarters of the bishop had been transferred from Shortland to Kieta. Up to that point the Marists, mostly of French and German nationality, were the only missionaries at work on Bougainville-Buka, but their exclusive hold on the field was soon threatened from the Solomon Islands where Methodists were reaching out towards the north.

Yet another kind of *waitman* presence on Bougainville-Buka during the German era which must be mentioned was the handful of journalists, scientists, traders and recruiters whose visits were brief but whose influence may have been considerable.

This was the situation in 1914, when World War I convulsed Europe, and its effects were felt even in distant colonies. shortly after the outbreak of war, Australian authorities rounded up a motley band of volunteer s and shipped them to Rabaul. their commander accepted the surrender of the handful of German residents, and announced to the bewildered crowds of onlooking indigenes: 'No more 'um Kaiser; God save 'um King'. this declaration revealed just how unprepared they and their political leaders were to govern this huge, alien, and seemingly intractable addition to empire.

From then until May 1921 the colony was administered by Australia under a military regime, but throughout this period most of the rules and practices established by the German s were continued. All German civilians taking an oath of neutrality were permitted to return to their properties and regular pursuits. such arrangements were not only in accord with the principles of international law of the time; they were also necessitated by the Australians' small numbers, their lack of tropical colonial experience, and their views on colonialism, which seem to have been almost identical with those of their predecessors.

After a while whites were deprived of the personal right to punish their indigenous employees corporally, but in most other respects the German-established laws and practices regarding relations between whites and indigenes were maintained. During this period of military occupation the colony came to be viewed as a protective bastion for Australia, but its natural resources and native peoples continued to be treated mainly as colonial economic assets.

The Australian force at Rabaul was so small that three months passed before it was able to extend the occupation to Bougainville-Buka. On 9 December 1914 two companies of infantry and a machine-gun section landed at Kieta without opposition and accepted the surrender of the German district officer there. the German officials were imprisoned and returned to Rabaul; other German residents - missionaries, planters and merchants - were permitted to return to their regular pursuits after taking the oath of neutrality.

A small military garrison was stationed at Kieta, but is main efforts throughout the occupation period were aimed at punishing fractious indigenes. Little was accomplished in the way of extending the areas under administrative control. Plantation and trading stores continued to operate as before, including even the German-owned ones, whose managers were allowed to remain.

By war's end, of the 30,000 hectares which had been alienated on Bougainville-Buka, including 1650 owned by the Marist mission, only one-third had been brought under cultivation. The only other major change that occurred during this period was brought about by missionaries. In 1911 the Methodist mission reached out from its New Georgia headquarters and established a station on Treasury Island, just south of the Shortlands. It would be hard to decide whether the Marists then put more energy into converting islanders from heathenism or saving them from the threat of Protestantism.

Some of the Marists were under the impression that the German authorities had granted their mission exclusive rights on Bougainville-Buka, this was not officially so, but until the Australian occupation the

Marists had the fiekd to themselves. From their base on Treasury Island the Methodists had made a brief sortie into the Siwai area of southern Bougainville in 1916, and then settled down to stay in 1920. Their entry there had been facilitated by the traditional relationship that existed between the Treasury Islanders and the Siwai; a similar factor had earlier provided the Catholic mission based on Shortland Island with entry into Buin.

Mandated Territory

As World War I drew to a close, Australia was faced with the question of what to do with German New Guinea, or rather, how to ensure the continuance of Australia's control there. It was officially recognized that the act of military occupation did not legally constitute the establishment of sovereignty, but it was widely assumed, and publicly demanded, that the colony would remain in Australian hands for both military and economic reasons. In Australia a few voices were raised against outright annexation, holding that it would be a betrayal of the Allied commitment to 'no territorial gains'.

A few others spoke up for the principle of 'self determination', implying that the colony's native populace should be consulted in the matter - an unrealistic proposal, to say the least! But when the Prime Minister, William Hughes, left for the peace conference in Paris, even most of the Opposition in the Australian parliament supported his wish to convert the de facto military control into outright sovereignty.

That development, however, was not to take place. In the face of the new anti-colonialist philosophy that prevailed at the peace conference, the best that Hughes could do was to have the former German New guinea proclaimed a ward of the new League of Nations, under mandate to Australia. As mandatory power, the Australian government agreed to administer the territory according to several general principles, including the undertaking to 'promote to the utmost the material and moral well-being and social progress of the inhabitants' (Article 2 of the mandate agreement).

In order to obtain expert advice on how to carry out its mandate, the Australian government appointed a royal commission to investigate and make recommendations. As it turned out, the recommendations of the commission served to shape events in the territory (including Bougainville-Buka) for the ensuing twenty years. The composition of the commission indicated at the outset what kinds of recommendations the government wished to have made, since the members' histories and attitudes concerning colonial matters were widely known.

The chairman was the top colonial official in the Territory of Papua, the veteran Lieutenant-Governor, Hubert Murray, a champion of indigenes' welfare. Lined up against him were W. H. Lucas, Island Manager for Burns Philp (the largest Australian mercantile firm then operating in the islands), and Atlee Hunt, Secretary of the Department of Home and Territories.

Papua, it will be recalled, had been under Australian administration since 1884. Because of its discouraging terrain, scattered population, and what then appeared to be meagre natural resources, Australian governments and Australian citizens in general showed little interest in developing Papua economically. some mining and plantation enterprise became established there, but under Murray's long governorship the Papua Administration gave first consideration to the indigenes' welfare.

Partly due to this policy and partly to geography, white businesses did not prosper as well in Papua as in neighbouring German New Guinea. In any case, Murray wished to extend this policy to the new Mandated Territory, and in fact to join the two territories into a united 'Papuasia'. (He also wished to become the first governor of the new union, but probably more out of a desire to extend the Papuan-style policy to it, than to advance himself personally.) As components of this policy he recommended nationalization of the German-owned properties (title to which had been awarded to Australia by the peace treaty); the leasing rather than the sale appropriated lands; and direct access to European and Asian markets in place of trans-shipment through Australian ports. These and similar measures were designated to favour development of a healthy, educated and affluent indigenous citizenry, even at the expense, if need be, of Australian enterprise.

For a variety of reasons the views of Lucas and Hunt, the majority, prevailed. The new Mandated Territory remained separate from Papua and plans made for its administration and development were aimed principally at furthering Australian national security and welfare. Australian attitudes differed, however, as to the best way to proceed. Some large firms active or interested in the Territory favoured the continuation and expansion of large-scale businesses there; other person, including members of the Opposition Labor Party, spoke up for dense colonization by independent white settlers.

(For political reasons both advocated that Australian war veterans be given preference for jobs and land in the Territory.) Throughout these debates and the actions that followed them, little or no attention was devoted to the cause of the indigenes themselves, either the matter was considered unimportant, or it was assumed that what was good for Australia was good for its colonial wards as well. s for the possibility that the indigenes of the new Territory would be treated humanely, it was asserted that the officials. Being Australian, would be incapable of acting otherwise.

Thus the principal and almost only concern of the new civil administration in the Mandated Territory (which assumed control in May 1921) was with Australian economic affairs. To begin with, all German-owned non-mission properties were expropriated and sold outright to Australians, by the terms of the peace treaty it was left to the German government to compensate its citizens for their losses. Most German missionaries were permitted to remain at their posts, but most other Germans were repatriated.

Many of the officials in the military administration doffed their uniforms and joined the civil administration. In many other respects, administrative policies and practices and Territory, had been brought under some measure of administrative influence or control. Established missions continued to widen their nets, and new mission bodies entered the field. Economically, coconuts continued for a decade to dominate, with the result that the whole Territory's money economy, including the Administration's revenue and expenditure, was strongly affected by rises and falls in the price of copra.

Later on, following the discovery of new ore beds around Wau, Bulolo and Edie Creek, gold mining became the principal revenue-producing industry of the Territory. Hundreds of whites and thousands of indigenes were employed in the new mining towns, which could be reached from the coast only on foot or by plane. By the end of the 1930s the major ore bodies had been nearly worked out, and since extensive exploration had turned up no other significant deposits of gold or any other minerals (including oil), it appeared that the Territory's future would, as in the past, depend upon agriculture.

This meant coconuts; other crops had been experimented with but abandoned, or proceeded with on a very small scale. By 1941 there were about 4600 whites in the Territory. About 10 per cent of these consisted of Administration personnel (including their dependants); another 15 per cent were associated with Christian missions; and nearly all the remainder were involved with plantations, mines, shopping and merchandising. The 2000 or so Asians in the Territory, mainly Chinese, were engaged largely in commerce. As for the indigenes, about 800,000 had been actually counted or their number estimated by 1941, with some parts of the mainland still largely unexplored. Meanwhile, the role of the indigenes in the Territory's developing economy had changed very little since the German era.

Although criticism had begun to be voiced both in New Guinea and Australia regarding the labour indenture system, it continued much as before. Many critics pointed to the anachronism in the twentieth century of a form of employment that was coercive, requiring government-enforced sanctions to keep labourers at their jobs throughout the term of their contracts.

Others criticized the low wages paid to the labourers, and the diet and living conditions found in plantation and mine labour-camps. Still others pointed out the harmful effects produced in the labourers' own communities by their long absences from home. No one, however, was able to propose a workable alternative, given the nature of the territory's economy and the requirement that the Administration pay for itself.

The Territory's agricultural economy - consisting mainly of copra production by crude technological means - depended upon large and constant amounts of cheap manual labour. Moreover, since most plantations were located far from the areas where most of the prospective labourers lived, and since the latter possessed neither the knowledge nor the means to travel to distant places of work, the cost of recruiting and transport had to be bone entirely by the employers. Under these circumstances it appeared at the time that few plantations could have maintained production and remained solvent without some form of enforceable labour contract. In the Territory as it then was, physical coercion was thought to be the only means of achieving that.

Critics of labourers' diets and living conditions were also rebutted with the item of coast, and with the observation that the living conditions were no more primitive than the ones the labourers were accustomed to at home. Employers were also able to point to the improvement in health experienced by many labourers under plantation regimes. On the other hand, so one could deny nor offer cures for the unhealthy social conditions that obtained in the compounds of labourers cut off from women and from most other interests and activities of their usual ways of life. Homosexuality and gambling were common, as were drunkenness and brawling; but worse than these in long-term effect were the kinds of attitudes such a life fostered in both employers and employees, between whites and indigenes.

As its best, the 'master-boy' relationship was tinged with feelings of paternalism and dependency, neither conducive to partnership. And at its worst, it was characterized by contempt, fear, envy and hatred. As for the widespread argument that employment on waitmans plantations served to inculcate valuable attitudes towards work and to introduce indigenes to other aspects of civilization as well: the jobs most of them performed would have produced only profound boredom and distaste, and the little bit of civilization they saw, from a distance, was not always edifying, and almost entirely inaccessible. Moreover, except for the blankets, knives, lanterns, etc., and their scant wages (most of which were used eventually to pay head taxes for themselves and their relatives), the things earned or learned on plantation were of little use in their lives at home.

At the height of large-scale gold dredging, many thousands of indigenes were employed at the Wau-Bulolo mines. Although the work there was more diversified and the white communities larger, the lives of the indigenous labourers, and the things earned and learned, were not very different from those of the plantation workers. As for the effects of the indenture system upon the labourers' home communities, some areas became so denuded of able-bodied males that regulations were imposed to restrict recruitment from them.

The absence of many men for long periods of time did not perhaps lead to any long-term population decline as some officials feared, but in some instances it did disrupt family and village life to a demoralizing degree. However, for all its adverse effects upon the Territory's indigenes, the indenture system cannot be judged solely from that point of view. while it did protect employers from labour desertions, it also protected the labourers from periodic lay-offs and arbitrary dismissal. While it took many labourers far from home, it also ensured their eventual return at the employer's expense.

Government taxation did undoubtedly force many otherwise unwilling indigenes to become labourers - the only means most of them had for earning tax money. But perhaps just as many sought employment, voluntarily and eagerly, for reasons of their own: to experience a new kind of life, to earn money for buying enticing new things, and to escape troubles at home.

During the mandate, the Administration imposed a tax on most adult male indigenes reassigning in 'taxable' areas, i.e. in areas that were firmly controlled and deemed economically capable of supporting the tax. In 1938-9, for example, 42,000 indigenes in the Territory paid the tax, out of an enumerated adult male population of 241,600. Several categories of persons were exempted, however: village officials; those individuals currently under indenture; mission teachers and students; fathers of four or more living children by one wife; and those physically unfit (which generally included all men judged to be over forty years old.)

In retrospect the tax seems rather high, since it represented about 10 per cent of the average indentured labourer's annual cash wages; but with all its exemptions it was levied on less than 20 per cent of the total enumerated adult male indigenous population of the Territory. Moreover, although it undoubtedly served to impel many indigenes into the ranks of indentured labour, and thus to support white enterprise, its official purposes were more widely developmental and educational: it was viewed as a device for encouraging indigenes to take up cash-crop production and to adopt responsible attitudes towards citizenship. In fact, while the measure may have had a small but positive measure of success in fulfilling the former objective, it failed altogether in relation to the latter.

Throughout the period of the mandate the civil authorities maintained almost unchanged the system of local government established by the Germans. As soon as an area was brought under control a chief (luluai, kukerai), interpreter (tultul), and medical orderly (doctorboy) were appointed in each of its indigenous communities. In some places an effort was made to encourage larger administrative units by placing several communities and their local officials under the supervision of an appointed paramount (number one) chief (nambawan luluai), but usually such measures proved effective only in places where they served to consolidate traditional tribal groupings. In addition, even larger multi-tribal councils were encouraged in more Europeanized Rabaul and Morobe, but otherwise the Territory's indigenous population remained as administratively atomized and politically voiceless as before.

Rabaul continued to be the Territory's capital throughout the mandate era, even after gold mining and the opening up of vast new areas to control had served to raise the mainland to greater commercial and administrative importance. At the top of the governmental hierarchy was an administrator and three departments - secretariat, public health and native affairs. In practice, because of great distances and infrequent communications, most governing was left to officials in each of the Territory's seven districts (of which Bougainville, Buka, Nissan, Nukumanu, Tauu, Kilinailau, and Nuguria constituted one).

The Christian missions supplied their indigenous members with some medical aid, but most health services, such as they were, were provided by the Administration. Each district had its government hospital, but these were able to serve only a very small proportion of the indigenes requiring medical care. In addition, European medical officers made periodic, usually annual, tours of outlying areas, but were able to attend to only the most obvious, and current afflictions. As for all the other maladies which shortened and made painful the lives of the Territory's indigenes, few preventive or therapeutic measures could be undertaken by an Administration having so few medical or public health resources at its command.

An even drearier picture is presented by the Administration's education programme, if it can be so dignified. There were only six government-operated schools for indigenes (four on New Britain, one on New Ireland, and one on the mainland), comprising in 1940-1 a total of 466 pupils of an estimated total population of 800,000. In fact, the Administration, with its limited resources, seemed more than content to leave schooling in the hands of the missions - an arrangement with which the latter evidently agreed.

Some 70,000 pupils were enrolled in mission schools during 1940-1, but the impressiveness of this number must be deflated somewhat, since most of these pupils were in sub-primary village schools, where instructions was rudimentary and casual, to say the least. Before turning more specifically to Bougainville-Buka, some explanation should be offered as to why so little headway was made by Australia in carrying out its mandate to 'promote to the utmost the material and moral well-being and social progress' of the Territory's indigenes.

Anyone familiar with the Territory during the mandate era could not blame the Administration itself over much for the failure to live up to the mandate. Administration forces undoubtedly indicated many individuals who were 'coon-bashers' through ignorance or calculation; but there were many more who viewed the indigenes with liking and sympathy, and worked faithfully, even heroically, on their behalf. Nor should one blame the white settlers overmuch for the plight of the indigenes. Coon-bashers were probably not as numerous among the ranks of plantation managers, recruiters and traders, but among these were also numerous individuals of fairness and goodwill. Moreover, the latter had their own livelihoods to earn, under conditions wherein low labour costs were essential for economic survival - or so the prevailing theory held.

In retrospect one must hold the policy-makers in Melbourne and Canberra, and ultimately the Australian voters as a whole, responsible for the shortcomings in indigenous welfare and progress. It was they who set the policy of requiring the Territory to pay for itself on a year-to-year basis. Such a policy could have yielded more immediate resources for education, etc., by granting subsidies as investments; but this was not done to any significant degree.

The inevitable consequence of these official policies is indicated by the fact that the Administration's annual expenditure - which derived almost entirely from imports and other forms of local taxation -

remained between 450,00 pounds and 500,000 pounds. Of this only about one-third (by the most liberal estimate) was spent on matters described as 'essentially native'; in other words, some 150,000 to 170,000 annually among an enumerated population of over 800,000! No wonder that the harassed Administration was pleased to accept the Christian missions' assistance in matters of health, and mission substitution in matters of education .

By the operation of this requirement that the Territory pay for itself, the indigenes were brought to the boundaries of civilization, white style, but were fated not to cross. In 1941 there were about 175 non-indigenous (white and Chinese) adults residing on Bougainville and Buka. Of these, about half were associated with Christian missions, and the remainder with plantations, retail stores, a small gold-mine at Kupei, and the administration. The indigenous population of that period is more difficult to characterize and quantify.

According to the census of 1941 there were about 45,000 indigenes residing in native settlements on Bougainville-Buka, and another 3000 residing in European enclaves, mainly plantations. Virtually all of the former were locally born; of the latter, most were locally born, and the remainder had come from other parts of the Territory. Fin ally, the statistics for that period record that some 850 locally born Bougainvillians were working and residing elsewhere in the Territory.

By themselves these figures provide little sociological information, they need to be supplemented by facts of another kind. Firstly, not one of the indigenes occupied a position of authority or social status equal to that of any of the whites with whom they associated in administrative, commercial or religious organizations. And secondly, although many had been conditioned to wish for it, not one indigene was able to match any of the whites in the attainment of a Western-style standard of material well-being. In other words, after many decades of contact with whites, including two decades of officially pledged noblesse oblige, the native proprietors of these islands had been obliged (or at least encouraged) to give up many of the satisfactions of their old ways of life without being able to taste the fruits of the newhe limbo in which they were stranded contained a poignant juxtaposition of old and new.

By 1941 every part of Bougainville-Buka had been visited by Administration officials and declared to be 'under control'. Most indigenous settlements of any size had been located and their populations counted or estimated. High up on the slopes of the northern Emperor Range lived people to whom the sight of a white was a rare event, but even th4ese had learned to acknowledge the latter's superior power and to want some of their goods. Kieta remained the administrative headquarters for the whole district, with sub-district headquarters at Sohano (Buka Passage) and Kangu (Buin coast).

Among all these centres there were half a dozen officials, along with several 'police boys' (indigenous members of the Territorial police force). They issued rules, judged all but the most serious of civil and criminal cases, punished malefactors, supervised labour contracts, and carried out periodic tours to record census changes and collect taxes. In addition to a body of criminal law, which applied to indigenes and all other residents as well, there went numerous native regulation s concerned with everything from sorcery and adultery, upon a handful of whites of widely varying capabilities and temperaments. consider the caser of southern Bougainville.

In 1938 the Buin sub-district contained an indigenous population of 16,500 indigenes, scattered over about 3100 square kilometres of difficult terrain accessible only by footpath or bicycle trail. At that time another 1200 to 1300 residents of the sub-district were working and living elsewhere, mainly under indenture. four different languages were spoken in the sub-district, none of them ever having been systematically recorded in published grammars or dictionaries.

Though alike in some respects, many customs of the sub-district's populace varied even more widely than their languages, and only a few years previously the whole region had been given by local feuding and warfare. such was the realm which one official, usually of very junior rank, was required to govern: to count its people, collect taxes from them, introduce them to an alien set of rules, police them, adjudge them, and punish them. In addition, this official was frequently required by circumstances to arbitrate conflicts involving indigenous customs about which he knew next to nothing and was insufficiently trained to investigate.

And all of this had to be done by means of a lingua franca, Pidgin, which was quite incapable of conveying many nuances of meaning from native vernacular to English or vice versa. No wonder that many Administration officials regarded their indigenous wards as contrary and stupid, or that the latter came to view the kiap (captain) as arbitrary and inscrutable.

One of the more arbitrary and incomprehensible measures undertaken by kiaps on Bougainville-Buka was to create large nucleated villages where they had not previously existed. The most characteristic settlement pattern in pre-European times consist4d of small hamlets of one of four household; each was located near its members' grove s and gardens, and separated by some hundreds of metres from other such settlements.

In some coastal areas somewhat larger and denser settlements were found, but the bulk of the pre-European population of Bougainville-Buka was widely and thinly scattered, In order to facilitate administration, the Australian officials brought together the people of neighbouring hamlets and required them to build 'line-villages', consisting of straight rows of narrowly spaced houses surrounded by a village fence made strong enough, hopefully, to exclude pigs (and thus help keep the villages 'clean'). Whenever possible these line-villages were designed to incorporate hamlets of people sharing close kinship ties, and so many of them were and have since remained. In other instances, however, the officials juxtaposed kin units and individuals who had no interest in being together, with the result that such people occupied their line-villages only during the infrequent visits of the kiap and lived the rest of the time in their hamlets.

As in the rest of the controlled parts of the Territory, the Administration maintained on Bougainville-Buka the system of organization introduced by the Germans, wherein each village was placed under the supervision of a kukerai, a tultul, and a doctorboy. All three of these village officials were appointed by the area's Australian Administration officer, or kiap, although an effort was usually made by the latter to conform to popular choice in the naming of the kukerai.

In some places one local resident was so prominent that the selection offered no difficulty. In other places rival factions made the choice more difficult and it had to be resolved by a vote - i.e., an alien and not always satisfactory way of resolving differences. In still other places, where the whole alien institution of gavman (government) was viewed with suspicion or outright hostility, the locally recognized leaders caused some henchman to be appointed kukerai, and then proceeded to rule as before, unencumbered by the obligation and conspicuousness attached official appointees.

In mist parts of Bougainville-Buka the villages were grouped by the Administration into large units, each under the supervision of an appointed nambawan luluai, and his interpreter-executive officer (bossboy). These two officials served mainly as links between village officials and the Administration. In some instances they exercised considerable authority, with or without the boundaries of their own village. All of the officials were exempt from paying head tax, and in addition a nambawan received an annual salary of sixty shillings. All of them were presented with peaked caps to wear when carrying out their official duties, hence their label of hat-men.

Village officials were responsible for maintaining law and order in their communities; for keeping a record of births, deaths, arrivals and departures; for constructing and maintaining the portion of the Administration road that passed through their areas; for supporting European travellers with porters along assigned stretches of road; for sending the sick and wounded to hospitals; and for carrying out any other duties that might be imposed by their numbawan. 'Maintaining law and order' was a broad mandate indeed.

Specifically the village kukerai was charged to 'arrest natives belonging to their tribes or villages whom they suspect to be guilty of wrongdoing or an offence', and to 'bring them to the nearest court in the district, or before the district court, to be dealt with according to law'.

The courts in question were those presided over by Administration officials. Theoretically the indigenous officials were not permitted to try cases or execute judgements; actually many of them did, with or without the tacit consent of white officials. The actions that constituted offences or wrong-doing were numerous and comprehensive, including, for example, gambling, sorcery and threats of sorcery, use of intoxicating liquor, 'careless use of fire', unsanitary practices, burying bodies too near to dwellings, behaving in a riotous manner, using obscene language, spreading 'false reports tending to give rise to trouble or ill feeling amongst the people or between individual', and the wearing (by males) of clothes over the upper part of the body. In other words an undigested mixture of Australian laws, public hygiene guide-lines, and Victorian pruderies.

Not surprisingly, the opportunities for abuse of authority under such a regime were numerous. The Administration of course regulated against this situation as well, as in the following:

> Any luluai, kukerai, tul-tul, patrol medical tultul (doctorboy) or other native upon whom the government has conferred authority, who uses such authority for the purpose of blackmail or wrongfully to get any property or benefit for himself or any other person or wrongfully to injure any other person shall be guilty of an offence.
>
> Penalty: Three pounds or six months imprisonment, or both.

In the long run, however, local indigenous sanctions were probably more effective than Administration regulations in checking such abuses, provided that the victims knew enough about the regulations to realize that the hat-men were in fact exceeding their authority.

Portering was not required of Bougainvillians very frequently - perhaps three or four times a year in most areas - but it was nevertheless un popular. Even the relatively high payment received, a twist of tobacco for about two to three hours' work, did not serve to make such work any less distasteful.

Even more unpopular was the construction work required periodically on most men. This consisted mainly of building and maintaining roads, bridges and rest houses (for whites). In the Buin Plains region of southern Bougainville where the writer observed it most closely, this activity required a large amount of the indigenes' time. The age-old trails there which served the purpose of foot travel were considered by the Administration to be too narrow and circuitous.

To facilitate patrolling, the Administration obliged the indigenes to construct straight trails some 2.75 metres wide and suitable wherever possible for bicycle travel. Bridges were ordered to be constructed over the smaller steams, and these were required to be roofed over to prolong the life of the spans. At intervals along the road network, rest houses were built to house Administration officials and other white travellers.

The original work for these projects involved weeks of labour, but maintenance would have required only a few hours' work a week of every adult male had it not been for the ambitions of some indigenous officials. In order to curry flavour with the Administration, some officials caused their stretched of road to be widened, graded and smoothed - all by hand and machete - for beyond the standards yet by the Administration. Bridge timbers were shaped and planed as flat as a floor - first-rate carpentry but hardly necessary for their infrequent use. The climax to such endeavours was reached with the rest houses. A small one-or two-room affair would have served well enough, but in some villages the indigenous officials ordered enormous barn-like structures to be built, up[to twenty-seven metres long and suitable for permanent residence of a whole troop. In such instances the competition which characterized indigenous politics was carried into the new activities, and many *kukerai* endeavoured to built bigger and better than their rivals elsewhere.

A head tax of ten shillings a year would appear at first glance to be burdensome for men with so little opportunity to earn Australian currency. Actually the exemptions were so numerous that the burden was spread quite thinly; of the whole adult male population of Bougainville-Buka, only about one in three had to pay. Nevertheless this did not make taxation any less unpopular. Administration officials were at pains to explain the impost in terms of the theory of 'taxation for responsible citizenship', but it is doubtful that this logic was widely understood, much less accepted.

Even those few indigenes who comprehended the general theory seemed to feel that it hardly applied to them; aft4er all, they did not elect the Administration officials nor participate to making the rules. Also, many Bougainvillians were heard to express resentment that whites with their great treasures of money should take away money from indigenes who had so little. Finally, although it may not have been officially intended that taxation would force Bougainvillian s to work, and thereby serve white commercial enterprise, it often had that effect.

Alongside the governmental structure imposed by the Administration, there continued to exist numerous indigenous ones; some had lines of authority that corresponded to the local administrative hierarchy and others had an entirely separate leadership. In places where the two systems corresponded, where the indigenous-type leader was himself the *kukerai*, or where the *kukerai* was the true leader's henchman, village affairs went smoothly.

But where the true leader and the *kukerai* were rivals, which was quite often the case, the village was continually troubled with factionalism. Before the Europeans arrived and for some time thereafter, every coastal village and every neighbourhood grouping of hamlets constituted an autonomous political unit, a 'tribe'. There were hundreds of such tribes, and they varied widely in cohesiveness, depending upon the strength of their leadership. Also, there were differences in the routes to leadership.

In some tribes the leader inherited his position. This tended to be the mode in tribes dominated, numerically and economically, by a single matrilineal kin group. In other tribes the leader achieved his position by attracting followers through personal attributes of generosity and forcefulness. And finally, some leaders of both types succeeded from time to time in extending their authority over neighbourhoods beyond their own, this was usually accomplished by the exercise of military leadership which was occasionally, but not necessarily, linked with personal military prowess.

After the consolidation of Administration control, indigenous intertribal warfare was brought to a halt, but many of the old tribal groupings persisted. They were deprived of their military aspects but continued to function in other respects, for example as land-clearing and feast-giving teams, and as the unit within which wrongs were righted by informal means. In some cases, such tribal groupings were maintained, and even strengthened, in the form of the new line-villages. In other cases they were subdivided and effectively destroyed by the new line arrangement. In still others they persisted, despite having had their membership consigned to different 'lines'. This persistence of old tribal groupings in the face of the abolition of warfare and of Administration regrouping was mainly the result of the remarkable durability of one particular type of indigenous leadership: the type personified by men who achieved rather than inherited their positions of influence and authority.

This institution merits a closer look. Variations of it were found throughout Bougainville-Buka during he mandate era, the one best known to the author having been practised in the Siwai region of southwest Bougainville:

> Throughout the (Siwai) area, 'renown' was a very concrete concept; it meant, literally, the kind of esteem enjoyed by the man who gives feasts frequently. The concept was most elaborately institutionalized in the northeast quarter of the Motuna-speaking region, which, significantly, was not the richest part of the Plain in material surpluses. Here, at the centre of this complex of ideas and practice4s was the *mumi*, the man of the neighourhood who had most renown.

To become a *mumi* a man had to own or control material resources. He could either accumulate these by his own hard labour, plus the labour of members of his household, or he could persuade kinsmen and friends to make him gifts or extend him loans. he usual method of accumulating wealth was by cultivating large gardens and converting the surplus produce into pigs, which could then be either distributed at feasts or sold for shell money. Another method was b y making and selling pottery, another by practising magical skills for fees.

Accumulation alone did not however bring renown; wealth had to be distributed in the form of food and other valuables, usually at feasts. It was useful to have had a *mumi* father, to have begun life with some of the latter's reflected renown, together with what was left of his wealth after most of it has been given away in the form of mortuary distributions. such an initial advantage prompted many informants to assert that 'Only the son of a *mumi* can become a *mumi*.' Actually, a *mumi*'s son was only slightly better off than an orphan. He had to increase his inheritance many times over, or have very liberal backers, before he could begin serious feast-giving.

It is little wonder that the feast-giver was highly esteemed. Feast food - roasted and steamed pork, boiled eel and opossum, tasty vegetable and nut puddings - provided a welcome br4eak in the everyday monotony of a vegetarian diet. Also, natives keenly enjoyed the excitement of milling crowds and the pleasure of dancing and pan-piping. However, the ambitious man did not merely invite a few of his neighbours and treat them to a banquet: that would have been a waste of resources. He usually made the fest the occasion for a house-raising or some other kind of work-bee; no one esteemed him any less for that.

It was customary to begin a social-climbing, renown-seeking career by building a club-house. The club-house is a rectangular, shed-like structure built directly on the ground and without walls. Large wooden slit-gongs occupy most of the floor space. These are sounded to convene workers, to announce feasts, etc., and serve as benches for the men who gather in the club-house to gossip and sleep.

Here among these Siwai only kinfolk visited one another's hamlet dwellings, so that the club-house was virtually the only public gathering place for men. Hence, the man who wished to become *a mumi* had to own a club-house; and to derive most renown for his ownership of one he had to build it rather than inherit it. The most renown-bringing manner of building a club-house was to collect all the helpers available, draw out the work as long as possible, and reward the workers with such a bountiful feast that they would ever aft4erward remember the occasion and the club-house with pleasure.

There were many club-houses in the Siwai region in the thirties - an average of one to about eight adult males - so that mere possession of one did not ensure for the owner lasting renown. To serve as a lasting symbol of the owner's renown, the club-house had to be the scene of almost continuous activity, and since nothing drew or pleased a crowd like a fest, the ambitious owner gave as many feasts as he and his followers could afford.

He had men cut down trees, fashion them into slit-gongs, and install them in the club-house; then he rewarded them with a pork feast. When no more gongs could be crowded into the club-house, he caused the roof to be repaired or the floor swept, and provided food delicacies for each occasion. After a while people would say of him: 'He is a true *mumi*: he gives large feasts.' And when they strolled about in search of amusement they would usually end up in his club-house.

They were at pains to ingratiate themselves with the feast-giver, to defer to his judgement, to perform little services for him, laugh at his sallies of wit, praise whom he praised or scorn whom he scorned. In this manner the *mumi* assured himself of a following in his own neighbourhood and even extended his renown and influence beyond.

Some *mumis* stopped there; others were led by their ambition to seek wider acclaim. Their lives turned into continual rivalries for renown. so long as they were active fest-givers they could count on exercising authority over their immediate neighbours and kinsmen, who lined up behind them with patriotic pride in 'our *mumi*' and 'our place'. Those rivalries between neighbouring *mumis* culminated in competitive '*mumi*-honouring' feasts at which the host presented his rival with large quantities of pigs and shell money.

The guest of honour then distributed these goods among his own supporters, as rewards for their support, and then set about to accumulate an equivalent or more than equivalent reciprocal gift. If he could not reciprocate within a year or two he forfeited much public esteem and was no longer considered a worthy rival by other *mumis*. If he returned an equivalent amount of goods and no more, that was a sign that he wished to cease competing with the initiating host; thereafter the two usually became 'trade-partners and assisted one another in competing with other *mumis*. If, however, the debtor-guest reciprocated more than he received, the rivalry continued until one of the principals gave up in defeat.

A supernatural sanction supplemented the social sanctions connected with these exchanges either the club-house demon-familiar or an ancestral spirit of the creditor *mumi* accompanied the 'gift' and tore out the soul of the debtor *mumi* if he did not repay in good time. (In my experience, however, this supernatural sanction provided less motive power than the social ones.)

A successful *mumi* was fortunate in a number of respects. he was singled out among his fellows by means of special beliefs about his personality and destiny - for example, the *mumi* had a better chance than most other mortals of attaining paradise. Also, he had the satisfaction - highly valued among these people - of hearing himself frequently praised. Others showed great respect for his name and person and opinion s, and in his own community he exercised considerable authority even in matters not directly concerned with feast-giving. Next to his material resources his most powerful weapon was his ability to focus [raise or scorn upon fri3nds or enemies.

There were also certain more material advantages in being a *mumi*. It other men's pork distributions a *mumi* usually received the best cuts. He had little difficulty in raising loans. And he had the tacit right to utilize land belonging to all those persons to whom he regularly distributed pork or other valuables. The term *tuhia* was applied to these persons and, derivatively, to the lands so utilized by them; it was in this connection that natives describe certain *mumis* as having had extensive *tuhias*, which some whites had interpreted as 'kingdoms'.

There were also drawbacks in being a *mumi*. Such a man had to be scrupulous in his everyday conduct and in his commercial or ceremonial transactions. Moreover, he was dangerously situated, in being the potential victim of sorcery aimed at him by envious rivals. Informants stated that in the days before the German and Australian control *mumis* were primarily war-leaders, their renown having been mainly dependent upon their success in organizing and financing victorious head-hunting forays or pitched battles with rival *mumis*.

In those day, informants asserted, a *mumi's* authority was backed by physical force. How closely such assertions corresponded to past actual events it is difficult to judge, but even according to these supposition, feast-giving was the principle kind of reward given by a *mumi* to his warriors, and fest-giving was the most important factor during the early stages of a man's rise to affluence. Feast-giving rather than personal bravery or martial skill attracted followers who would then fight one's battles.

By 1941 German and Australian control had succeeded in ending inter-tribal warfare, thereby removing much of the basis for the traditional form of tribalism. The Germans and Australians had also imposed a new form of territorial grouping and leadership, which conformed only in part to traditional tribal boundaries and forms of leadership. yet desp0ite all the coercive authority behind the Administration's *kukerai* system, it was unable in many places to supersede the traditional form.

By 1941 Australians had also attempted to creat4e larger indigenous groupings, but these units, under so-called 'paramount chiefs' or *nambawans*, were in fact more ceremonial than administrative, and seem not to have fostered any sense of wider political boundaries. After several years of decades of contact with whites, the indigenes exercised less control over their own lives than ever before. Despite having become members of a vastly larger and purportedly more democratic 'tribe', they had little or no voice in their own governing.

Nor did they acquire any sizeable stake in the new capitalistic market economy of their islands during he mandate era. By 1937 whites had alienated 28,000 hectares of Bougainvillians' land, nearly all of it of prime agricultural quality and accessible to shipping points. Of this, over 10,500 hectares were planted in coconuts and most of the remainder was designated for coconut planting. Figures on total copra production on Bougainville-Buka are not known, since they were not segregated from Territory corals in published reports. However, it is safe to say that most of the copra exports were produced on white-owned plantations.

Some indigenes in central areas sold self-grown and self-processed copra to traders, but this constituted a small percentage of the two islands' exports. Nor did the Administration attempt much in the way of encouraging indigenes in cash-cropping. One or two officials, on their own initiative required the men in their sub-districts to plant coconuts when their wives gave birth as a means of ensuring 'family welfare', but this was a sporadic enterprise and was not followed up with assistance in processing and marketing.

Locally made handicrafts included the now famous 'Buka' baskets (which were in fact made in southern Bougainville). Such handicrafts provided a few indigenes with some cash, but the volume was small and the prices low (for example a large bowl-shaped basket fetched only a few shillings). Up to 1941 no official effort had been made to encourage this potential profitable form of indigenous enterprise.

And finally, virtually all retailing remained in white or Chinese hands. Now and then a hopeful Bougainvillian invested his wage savings in a small stock of goods for resale to his neighbours, but such enterprises were usually very short-lived, and received no technical or financial assistance from the Administration. In other words, during the mandate era about the only part played by Bougainvillians in their islands' developing market economy was as wage labourers in white enterprises.

Some Bougainvillians were employed as casual labourers, but for the largest population of wage labourers worked under indenture, principally as unskilled labourers on plantations. In 1939, for example, there were about 3400 working under indenture, about 2500 worked on Bougainville-Buka itself, and the remainder elsewhere in the Territory. At that time there were also 131 indigenes from elsewhere in the Territory working under indenture on Bougainville-Buka.) It would be pertinent to inquire what these labourers gained, economically or socially, from this, their closest and most sustained contact with whites.

Assuming that the average wage of each labourer was 3 pounds a year (the wage for unskilled labour was between six and ten shillings a month), wage earners would have earned during 1939 about 17,000 pounds. By viewing this as income for Bougainvillians as a whole, and subtracting from the figure some 2400 pounds (the approximate amount of head tax collected on Bougainville-Buka that year), this would leave about 34,600 pounds for other purposes, or about six shillings per capita per annum, i.e. enough to buy a strip of calico, a few pounds of rice, and a few sticks of trade tobacco.

But what about other benefits? Mention has already been made of some of the detrimental consequences of the indentures-labour system; the irrelevancy to indigenous life of most plantation-acquired skills, the unsavoury moral atmosphere of labour compounds, the psychological time of the master-boy relationship, the social disruptions in home life brought about by the workers' long absences, etc. on the other hand, the combination of medical care, muscular regimes and plantation food (monotonous as it was) does seem to have produced somewhat healthier individuals.

And, however divisive it may have been in other aspects, a term of labour in a white enterprise, especially plantations and mines, served to provide a model for a larger-scale indigenous society. Despite the interethnic conflict that occurred in many labour compounds and colonial towns - Buka Islanders against Buins, Sepiks against Bougainvillians, etc. - experience of working together, and in the same roles, may have served to dampen some of the intertribal hostility that characterized indigenous life in pre-white times. And finally, Pidgin, which most indentured labourers succeeded in learning, provides a means of communication across old tribal boundaries as well as with the alien Europeans.

Meanwhile, the subsistence economy of Bougainvilliains persisted very much as before. vegetable staples and gardening techniques remained unchanged. Indigenes were introduced to new crops, maize, tomatoes, beans and pawpaw. Some of the set they grew on a small scale, but mainly for sale to whites because most indigenes found each food unsatisfactory substitutes for their own taro, sweet potatoes and yams.

Many indigenes developed a taste for rice, but the sporadic efforts to grow it did not succeed and few people were willing to expend their precious little hoards of shillings for this kind of luxury. The change in meat supply was somewhat greater. Interbreeding with new strains considerably increased the size of local pigs, and made pig breeding a widespread preoccupation. On the other hand the increased production scarcely affected people's daily diets, since pork continued to be reserved for festive occasions. As in the case of rice, many Bougainvillians developed appetites for tinned beef and fish, but few were in a position to afford such luxuries.

In its efforts to introduce white notion s of public hygiene, the Administration required pig-proof fences around the new line-villages, and encouraged people to raise their dwellings off the ground on piles. (Pile dwellings were not unknown in pre-European times, but most dwellings were formerly built directly on the ground.) As a result of these efforts pile dwellings did indeed become more numerous, in line-villages that is; in their hamlets most people continued to live in their ground-level houses. As for other architectural innovations of the mandate era, very few indigenes were financially able to emulate whites to the extent of roofing their houses with metal.

By 1941 there were probably no indigenous households on Bougainville-Buka without a metal cooking pot or two, although many of them continued to see their own clay vessels. Few adult males were without a steel machete, and many of them owned steel axes or adzes as well. Just as universal were smoking pipes, both wood and clay, for women as well as men. A few Bougainvillians were able to afford an occasional stick of twist tobacco - at threepence apiece - but most of the tobacco used was house-grown (and wholly uncured).

In at least one respect the Administration's policy met with outstanding success. As part of its mandate undertaking, it pledged itself to discourage the consumption of alcohol by indigenes. Even after decades of observing the whites at this congenial pastime, few Bougainvillians followed suit. They were not permitted to purchase alcohol, and drunkenness was sternly penalized.

But perhaps more effective was the fact that few Bougainvillians were affluent enough to purchase beer, much less spirits. White notions of modesty were only partially diffused throughout the islands. Virtually every Bougainvillian past early childhood became accustomed to wearing a *laplap* - a strip of calico reaching from waist to below the knees - but mission efforts to induce the girls and women to cover their breasts met with only sporadic success.

It is possible, but difficult to document, that the Bougainvillians improved somewhat in physical health as a result of their twenty-year wardship. for example, all obvious cases of leprosy, tuberculosis, meningitis, etc. were hospitalized, and both Administration and mission agents conducted campaigns against yaws. Also, as previously noted, a term of years spent on plantations seems to have had a generally good effect upon the indigenous labourers, in terms of physical well-being at least.

On the other hand, little progress appears to have been made in eradicating such major killers as malaria and pulmonary diseases. As for mental health, although there is no evidence of increase in extreme forms of mental illness, the period spent under mandate rule can only have increased the psychological stresses occasioned by insubordination to incomprehensible authorities and ways of life. By 1941 nearly all Bougainvillians had become at least nominal adherents to Christianity, of one variety of another, and some had even begun to develop new varieties of Christianity of their own.

At the beginning of the Australian military occupation in 1914 the Marist mission maintained four stations on Bougainville (Kieta, Patapatuai, Koromira and Torokina) and one on Buka Island at Burunotui, and counted some 800 to 900 baptized converts on the two islands. By 1939, the last pre-war year for which there are figures, the number of Marist mission stations had increased to twenty-one and the number of converts to over 30,000, including over 25,000 baptized members and over 5000 catechumens and adherents.

Ministering to this large flock were twenty-nine priests, six brothers, twenty-five sisters and five lay nurses, all white, and seven indigenous sisters. To appreciate the great numerical weight of these sixty-five or so white Catholic missionaries, they should be compared with the numbers of other non-indigenous adults living on Bouagainville-Buka at that time: six Methodist missionaries, two seventh Day Adventist missionaries, and some hundred other whites engaged variously in production, commerce, or the Administration. In other words, in terms of numbers alone Catholicism constituted the largest agent of social change in these two islands, and the most widespread manifestation of change. How deep seated a change it was remained to be seen.

Throughout the mandate era, the primary goal of the Marist mission appears to have been to save indigenes' souls, either from the darkness of paganism or the error of Protestantism. Individual missionaries undoubtedly ministered to the physical and material well-being of their changes, and in the course much mission-wide effort went into health care and education; but evangelism was the overriding objective.

The Marist strategy for carrying out its mission was to set up stations, staffed with priests, nuns and brothers, consisting of churches, schools, living quarters for the missionaries and pupils, vegetable gardens and, at the larger coastal stations, coconut plantations. The gardens were needed to feed the station personnel, and the plantations to help finance the whole mission enterprise. Some financial support came from outside sources, including funds raised by the missionaries themselves in their homelands, but much of the operating costs had to be paid for by profits from the missionaries' own commercial enterprises, a circumstance that added immeasurably to the mission's principal task.

The necessity to be as self-supporting as possible required of many missionaries that they devote too much time and energy to copra production, leaving too little for their evangelical teaching and pastoral duties. For labour they depended heavily upon their schoolboy boarders, who spent more time working than attending their lessons. The mission's acquisition of good agricultural land, however, 'voluntarily' tendered, sometimes entailed conflict with its indigenous neighbours and served to identify it with other kinds of *waitman* takeover. And finally, the mission's operation of plantations, in prime agricultural areas and with 'free' student labour, aroused protests from other white planters.

As remarked earlier, the Administration operated only a few schools, and none at all on Bougainville-Buka. In these islands indigenous education was left entirely in the hands of the missions, a task which the Marist mission was pleased to undertake and indeed zealously sought to monopolize. However, during the mandate, the mission's educational goals went no further than their evangelical ones: to save souls.

Beyond instructing new converts enough to prepare them for baptism, the only formal schooling was that given young boys at the station boarding-schools and was designed to turn them into village catechists. It was only towards the end of the era, and largely in response to a growing challenge from the Methodists, that one of the catechist schools (the one at Chabai) was placed in the hands of trained missionary educators. But even this move was intended mainly to increase the pupils' value to the central evangelical purpose of the mission. The Marist mission also supplemented the Administration's meagre medical services to Bougainvillians. Humanitarian sentiments undoubtedly played a part in this, but as in the case of education it appears that much of the mission's work was specifically undertaken to win converts or to avoid losing them to the Protestants.

How did the mission's primary task - that of conversion - take place, and how were the new converts incorporated into membership of the church? the normal procedure of conversion has been described by the historian, Hugh Laracy' his account is as follows:

The Marists, like all missionaries, generally found adult pagans - those most committed by habit and interest to old religious allegiances - reluctant to adopt Christianity. . . . therefore, children were regarded as the hope of the mission and the Marists' efforts were mainly directed to drawing as many as possible into the station schools, where study was a novelty, discipline generally light, calico and tobacco regularly obtained and the (pagan) spirits impotent.

> Pupils eventually received baptism almost as a matter of course. Normally, their catechumenate lasted about eighteen months. . . . Pupils usually returned, directly or via the plantations, to their villages. There some acted as teachers and prayer leaders, but most helped diffuse awareness of the *lotu* (Christian religious ritual) simply by their conversation, whetting the interest of their fellows with tales of what they had seen and learned. Infants were baptized whenever the parents approved. The baptism of adults, where there were no matrimonial impediments, was at the priest's discretion. A catechumenate of six months, including a period at the station, might be required to test an adult candidate's sincerity and to extend his knowledge of Christianity;

especially once mission influence became established in an area, a request was sufficient to obtain baptism. (Laracy 1976, p. 74)

Perhaps the most obdurat4 difficulty in winning adult converts was the mission's rule on marriage: only monogamous persons were eligible for baptism. Before a polygamous man -there were no polygamous women on Bougainville-Buka - could be baptized, he was required to put aside all but one of his wives.

This ruling was no obstacle to most men; although by indigenous custom any male could acquire as many wives as he would and could afford, only a few actually did so. But among those few were usually to be found the most affluent and influential men in the indigenous communities, and by excluding them from baptism the mission lost the drawing power of their example. On the other hand many polygamists did cast aside their extra wives in order to be baptized, thereby securing for themselves the promise of a place in heaven. It is not recorded what became of the discarded wives.

Other than the requirement of monogamy, conversion did not demand any radical changes in the converts 'lives. It was enough that they attend services and participate on occasion in the sacraments, it was not required that they understand these rit4es. In fact, the simple cosmologies and ritual practices taught to new converts were similar in many respects to those of the indigenous religions. In each of the native languages encountered on Bougainville-Buka the missionaries were able to find verb al concepts near enough in meaning to Christian ones for their purposes of teaching and preaching. For example, among the Siwai people their pagan creator spirit, called *Tantanu* (Maker) was appropriated by the Marists and Methodists to designate God; although the divine qualities attributed to the Christian *Tantanu* were considerably greater than those of the indigenous spirit of that name, the identification seems to have been acceptable to both sides.

As for the other major Christian figures, Jesus and the Virgin Mary were of course new concepts to the Siwai, but the Holy Ghost *(Mara Mikisa)* fitted easily into indigenous belief in the familiar form of a supernatural bird. A Siwai convert to Methodism once described to me the differences between Catholic and Methodist beliefs: 'The *Popi* (Pope, i.e. Catholics) talk a lot about Jesus' mother and a place called Roma, while we *Taratura* (Methodists) think mostly about Jesus Himself.'

As for mission doctrines about souls (before and after death) and about saints, these accommodated quite easily to indigenous b4liefs. The mission's criticism of evil spirits and indigenous magic served only to reinforce what the indigenes already believed; namely, that evil spirits are dangerous and that some magic can be deadly. The mission concept of sin was more difficult, and few Siwai even bothered to wonder about it.

On one occasion this writer succeeded in having three Siwai teachers, to Catholics and a Methodist, discuss the subject together, and they agreed on the following proposition: that sin accommodates within a person as do other evil things, forming a hard round object that lies in the stomach. Catholics can rid themselves of sin through taking communion, but Methodists have no special means of ridding themselves of it and hence have to take special care to avoid doing sinful things.

Except for polygamists then, conversions to the Catholic mission creed and membership in the church did not require a major change in the indigenes' thinking and living. But it did represent a conscious acceptance, however superficial, of something partly new; and it may be asked what persuaded so many people to covert?

Some of the earliest conversions were accomplished through purchase. For example when the Marist mission was becoming established on Shortland Island some indigenes, including a few from Bougainville-Buka, were obtained for work on the station (and of course religious schooling) by payment of goods or money to their relatives. To paraphrase Laracy (p. 75), purchase was a guaranteed means of obtaining an initial following and of creating a core of potential assistance: those who were purchased belonged to the mission.

In many other instances individuals who were originally attracted to mission stations for purposes of earning money were converted as a matter of course. Another means whereby individuals were attracted to the mission in the first instance then held within the fold, was by generous hand-outs of tobacco, calico, tools, etc. Religious medals were also passed out in huge quantities; the wearing of one seems to have given the recipients a feeling of adherence to the mission, even without baptism.

The incentive to conversion supplied by a few specific trade goods was increased for some by their comprehensive belief that Christianity in general, and Catholicism in particular, would somehow provide an unending supply of *waitmans* goods of all kinds, as witnessed by the boat-loads of objects that whites (who were nearly all Christians) continually received.

Medical aid was instrumental in winning many converts. The missionaries were called upon to dispense medicine and first aid as a regular part of their pastorates, and eventually the mission was obliged to establish hospitals in addition to the dispensaries attached to each mission station. quite apart from any gratitude that may have been elicited by these services, they also served to impress Bougainvillians with the superior 'magical' powers possessed by the missionaries, more powerful even than those of their own magicians and sorcerers.

In this connection, there are indications that some missionaries, in their evangelical zeal, did nothing to disabuse them of such beliefs. The motivation behind these endeavours undoubtedly included some genuine humanitarian solicitude, but a need to equal or outdo Methodist medical services also played a part.

Many others became converts in the first instance in order to attend school. In the view of many Melanesians, on Bougainville-Buka and elsewhere, the main basis of whites' superiority in material goods, weapons, etc., was to be found in their knowledge, and schooling was the key to such knowledge. An understanding of English, particularly, came to be regarded as an essential ingredient of that knowledge, this circumstance, reinforced by rivalry with the English-speaking Methodists, moved the Marists to place less emphasis on the use of native vernaculars in schools and services and to augment their

French- and German-speaking staff with missionaries from Australia, new Zealand and the United States.

Still another powerful incentive to conversion, especially in the mission's early days in these islands, was the protection, real or imagined, that it afforded against other white attacks or encroachments. On some occasions it was only a missionary's interception that spared some community from positive action by the Administration. On other occasions, a missionary was the only white willing and able to defend indigenes against other non-official white infringements and greed.

An instance of the former occurred in Buin in 1919-20 when mass conversion took place in response to a series of punitive expeditions by the Administration, which included the execution of some feuders for homicide. On this occasion gratitude to the missionaries for having successfully shielded many innocents from Administration retribution was mixed with realistic acknowledgement that Christianized indigenes had wisely remained aloof from the feud. In some areas whole communities became converted as a consequence of the conversion of an influential kinsman or local leader. And, as will be described, there were instances in which one of the factions of an ancient feud joined the ranks of the Catholics in response to seeing their enemies become Methodists, the reverse also took place.

Another incentive to conversion, individual or en masse, may have been contained in the indigenes' own belief - very widespread in Melanesia - about cargo *(kago)*, a millennium in which every wish would be fulfilled, especially those concerning a plentiful supply of good foods and reunion with deceased kin. In some instances the appearance of the affluent and seemingly supernatural whites was viewed as materialization of the prophecy; the missionaries' promises about heaven reinforced such views. Missionary preaching about the terrors of hell may also have influenced some people to covert, although theological arguments were probably less influential than mundane practical considerations in most conversions.

Finally, in attempting to explain why Bougainvillain s underwent conversion to readily and in such large numbers, one should not overlook the fact that Christianity was for them not an entirely distinctive institution. It was but one aspect of the whole complex of new - *waitmans* - objects and customs. during the early stages of their encounters with the *waitmans* way of life, the latter must inevitably have appeared overwhelmed.

it was somewhat later, and then only sporadically, that the idea emerged of selecting only some parts of the new to complement parts of the old. As noted earlier, the Methodists installed their first mission in 1920, after an abortive attempt in 1916. The 1920 salient was established in Siwai by indigenous teachers from the missionary station on Treasury Island, and this was followed in 1922 by one white and three Fijian missionaries who set up a station on the west coast of Buka.

In 1924 and 1926 other Methodist stations were established at Teop and Siwai respectively, and in 1931 were 'on trial for membership'. On Bougainville-Buka its strategy resembled the Marists' in some respects and differed in others. Like the Marists, the Methodists based their operations principally on stations somewhat isolated from the indigenous communities, where youthful converts boarded, worked, attended school, and generally led lives quite unlike their lives at home.

More so than with the Marist, however, the education of th4ese young coverts included training in agriculture and industrial arts. This concept of industrial missions was based partly on the policy that the Methodist missions should be largely self-sustaining economically, and partly on the view that the indigenous Methodist should be industrious (in the white sense) as well as pious.

The Methodists were more exacting than the Marists in their requisites for church membership; they were considerably less tolerant of 'heathen customs', more interested in Westernizing their converts' characters and not only their religious beliefs. The third Christian mission to become established was that of the Seventh Day Adventists, who began their evangelical work in 1926 in the village of Lavelai on the southeast coast of Bougainville.

Their progress was very slow; in 1941 they recorded only about thirty converts, all in the area around Kieta. This is not to be wondered at, because their membership requirements were even more stringent than the Methodists' and included the prohibition of tobacco, betel chewing, and the eating of crustaceans and pork. To forswear pork-eating was an especially onerous test of commitment. Meat in any form was a grand luxury to these islanders, and much of their traditional life revolved around pigs - raising them, exhibiting them, trading them, gift-giving them, and eating them on the most solemn or festive of occasions. (While being impressed with the persuasiveness of a mission able to secure so deep a commitment, one also wonders why such a radical deprivation was demanded.)

Ecumenism was not in fashion in these islands before World War II; in fact, a reading of early missionary reports and correspondence creates the impression that a soul matched from Methodism (or Adventism, or Catholicism) was felt to be an even greater victory than one lifted out of heathenism. The Marists were first on the scene, while their proselytizing rights were not legally exclusive, as some of them appear to have believed, they were bitter at what they considered Methodist encroachments, and speeded up their evangelistic activities like an urgent military campaign.

As for the Methodists (the Adventists being still too meagre in numbers to constitute a threat), although there were several pagan areas in which they could operate, they made so bold as to evangelize mainly in the heart of Catholic strongholds. The rivalry was most intense in southern Bougainville and is here described by Laracy (pp. 63-4):

> Feelings ran highest in Siwai. The Methodists, who eventually attracted half the population, were reinforced in 1928 by an influx of teachers from new Georgia. The Marists were ready for them. The year before Father Boch had equipped a squad of catechists in south Bougainville with bicycles in order that they might more

quickly visit threatened villages, challenge Protestant emissaries and report back to their priest.

In November 1928 he issued instructions that forceful catechists, 'even insufficiently trained ones', he placed in each village and station work subordinated to visiting, even if it means making the schoolboys 'a troop of peripatetic scouts accompanying the (priests) . . . from village to village'. Visiting Siwai two months later and observing the bitter sectarian competition, the Government Anthropologist, W.P. Chinnery, suggested to Boch that the missions reach a *modus vivendi*, only to be told, 'If the Protestants wish to have peace with us, let them go where we are not . . . where our influence is established . . . there will be fight for each individual village if necessary'.

Fighting did break out shortly afterwards; Methodists and Catholic factions destroyed each other's chapels at Osokoli and Hukuha. A judicial commission was appointed to investigate the situation and, though its only official outcome was the restriction in 1930 of the entry of 'foreign' Melanesian and Polynesian missionaries to the mandated territory, it did consider the Marists most to blame for arousing the animosity of their followers. The display of government interest in mission activities (and the threat of further action it was thought to contain) did, however, have a pacifying effect. Rivalry in Siwai continued into the 1930s but it was more discreet, and decreased as the number of people unconverted to one side or the other declined.

As this point it will be illuminating to go beyond general statements about mission programmes and statistics on conversion to inquire how far these mission activities, singly and in opposition, had affected indigenous life in the off-station Bougainvillian communities themselves. Again the Siwai area, where both Catholic and Methodist missionaries had been long at work and where their converts lived side by side, provides an example of that era:

> In matters of belief, then, mission influence has made little impact upon most Siwai. similarly, Christianity cannot be said to have changed many Siwai practices. It has caused some Methodists to give up productive work on Sundays, and it has encouraged many of the younger men, especially Methodists, to wear cleaner loincloths; but it has had little effect in curbing polygamy or in changing sex mores. It has discouraged the practice of image-sorcery - the carved wooden figures (*poripai*) used in this sorcery are condemned by the mission as being 'graven images' - but it

has probably had little inhibiting effect on other kinds of magical practice.

In fact, some zealous converts now use Bibles as magical aids in litigation, and most natives see no difference at all between, say, Catholic . . . christening and Siwai (pagan) baptism. some Methodists heed their missionary and inhume rather than cremate their dead relatives, but for most natives Christian rites of passage merely reinforce the native rituals.

More significant than their influence upon religious beliefs and practices have been the mission's effects on social structure. As a result of mission rivalry new lines of social cleavage formed or old lines of cleavage crystallized. Catholics and Methodists no longer burned one another's chapels but many tensions continued to exist.

By 1941 Catholics outnumbered Methodists in Siwai, not because of differences in doctrine or practice but mainly because white Catholic missionaries had been at the job there longer and more continuously than their Methodist counterparts. Some villages were entirely Catholic, others entirely Methodist, depending usually upon which missionary began his work there first.

Once the missionary had received consent from the highest-ranking local leader to construct a chapel and install a native evangelist, most of the leader's followers moved into his fold. Troubles began only when overzealous native evangelists tried to set up rival chapels in places already nominally affiliated. Many of these efforts were frustrated but some of them succeeded, with the result that there were many villages with both Catholic and Methodist congregations.

In such cases the smaller congregation, usually representing the later mission to have become established, was nearly always identified with one or two hamlet units, conversion or transfer of affiliation having followed kinship lines. In most instances when a whole hamlet unit changed missions it did so at the behest of one of its more influential members. for example, one such unit became Methodist when its senior male member became piqued after being advised by his Catholic priest not to acquire a second wife.

Another unit became Methodist after one of its brighter young men returned from indenture with glowing tales of the imagined practical advantages of learning arithmetic and bookkeeping, which Methodist schooling specializes in. . . . In some cases the division between Catholics and Methodists corresponded to long-standing political divisions, with whole neighbourhoods having purposefully embraced the sect opposite to that of their traditional enemies. . . .

The tendency towards sect-endogamy had some effect upon the maintenance of social cleavages between opposing congregations, but many inter-sect marriages took place, with one of the spouses usually joining the congregation of the other, depending upon the choice of residence. There were, however, a few steadfast mission members, usually men, who did not change sects when they moved to the places of their spouses, and these accounted for most cases of scatterings of sect A members in villages belonging predominantly to sect B . .

Lines of inter-sect division did not harden so long as a village's minority sect members did not band together into a definite congregational unit. Nor, in the case of relations between separate villages of opposing sects, did the fact of different mission membership create new cleavages or add significantly to cleavages already present; active religious hostility between separate villages seemed to have ended. In 1941, social cleavage between sects was mainly manifested in villages having opposing congregations, each with it on chapel and native evangelist.

Elsewhere there were whole villages associated exclusively with one or other of the missions, thereby sparing the local indigenes at least this consequence of whites' eagerness for their land or labour or immoral souls. To summarize, the three Christian mission at work on Bougainville-Buka during the mandate era differed from one another in many respects - in doctrines, goals and conversion, methods of proselytization etc. - but in one important respect they were alike.

They continued to be *waitmans* institutions, as basically colonial as the white-owned plantations and Administration enclaves. All important mission decisions were made by whites and nearly all mission material resources responded in whites' hands. What indigenization of Christianity there was received its impetus from the indigenes themselves, and in forms that were more than distressing to the white missionaries and other whites as well.

Such developments first came to the notice of whites in 1913. They started in a corner of Buka but have since encompassed much of that island and have appeared in many parts of Bougainville as well. In 1913 word reached Europeans on Buka that a resident of Lontis village, a pagan named Muling, was attracting a large following by his claim to be able to acquire *waitmans* goods through magic, all other kinds of effort to do so having failed. His message fell on receptive ears.

Before this event, buy Islanders had been in fairly frequent contact with whites for more than forty years. Large numbers of them had served as labourers, policemen, mission scholars, etc., and had come to use and want goods that would permit them to live more like whites, whom they at first greatly admired, and whom one report suggests they first believed to be returned ancestral spirits. In any case the cult swelled to such size that the German Administration, fearful of its potential. Arrested Muling and exiled him from the island.

The excitement aroused by Moling's prophecies died down under Australian rule, but his fellow Buka Islanders seemed not to have lost their appetite for *waitmans* goods and ways, so that the Marists were well received when they began active evangelism there a few years later. The missionaries may not have specifically promised the indigenes material wealth in return for conversion, but its quite likely that the latter read such promises into the missionaries' assurance about spiritual rewards. Thus, Sydney (Australia) was believed by the indigenes to be the future abode of the righteous' it was also known to be the source of most of the goods that reached Buka. Within a few years over 90 per cent of Buka's indigenous population had become Catholic.

Meanwhile, Catholic *lotu* (ecclesiastical services) began to serve purposes which the mission never intended. If the *lotu* worked for the missionaries in bringing what they wanted, some Buka Islanders reasoned, why should it not work for them and bring ships laden with goods? Armed with this argument another Buka Island, Pako, initiated a new movement to acquire the desired cargo. One of the leaders of this new movement was a Catholic catechist, but the principal one, Pako, along with his associate, the repatriated and durable Muling, were pagans, this form of *lotu* had evidently become disengaged from the mission itself.

Modelling their actions on the mission practices of approaching the divinity through saints, Pako and his associates employed their *lotu* in petitioning their own ancestral spirits for aid in bringing the desired cargo. People refurbished their burial grounds and spent nights there in prayer, and a mood of excitement prevailed in expectation of the arrival of the cargo which had been prophesized by Pako. Gardening and pottery-making ceased (why worked when the expected ships would bring all the food and utensils needed?), wharves and storehouses were built to receive the cargo.

The movement was a bizarre mixture of new and old. Many old indigenous customs were renounced, new white ones adopted, and equality with whites was proclaimed. At its peak the cult - for such it was with its strong religious emphasis - embraced some 5000 Bougainvillians; this was the largest grouping up to then to unite on these islands, and a sign of things to come.

Subsequently, when some of the cult's members attempted to claim goods landed for whites, the Australian Administration stepped in and exiled the leaders to Madang, where Pako himself subsequently died. After this the popular excitement subsided for a year or so, but was stirred up again by another Buka pagan, Sanop, who moved into Pako's residence in Malasang village and began receiving mysterious messages which he identified as coming from Pako's spirit, again promising cargo, but this time ominously anti-white in tone.

Again, however, the cult contained much from Christianity, including the rituals of *lotu*, regular church attendance, an d insistence upon monogamy (except for the cult leaders). But even though cult members continued to value the Marist priests' ritual powers (the local priest baptized 200 new converts including some Methodists on one visit to a cult stronghold, and 'Bishop' appeared along with 'Pako' on cuolt banners), the cult members otherwise distinguished between their brand of Christianity and the European mission itself.

When the movement spread to northern Bougainville it became more militantly anti-white. Then, when talk of 'liberation' was reinforced by a mass desertion of labourers from their plantation jobs, the Administration moved in again. The cult leaders were arrested, along with about 100 followers, and Pako's home was burnt down. Meanwhile too cargo arrived to offset the famine caused by the earlier cessation of gardening, and the disheartened people returned to their ordinary pursuits. With this the Pako-Sanop episode ended. Faith in cargo was revived a few years later when Japanese ships appeared - but that is another story.

World War II

The shock waves produced by World War II convulsed Bougainville at the time. At war's end the principal agents of colonialism - Australian Administration, Christian missions, and white-owned plantation and commercial firms-returned to re-establish their respective controls over indigenous affairs, but neither they nor the islanders were to remain as before.

The events of the war that had the most far-reaching local consequences were the following:

December 1941. Japan attacks Pearl Harbor and moves towards Australia and the Pacific.

January 1942. The Japanese occupy Rabaul and attack Buka.

March 1942. The Japanese occupy Tulagi, British Solomon Islands.

August 1942. The United States forces land on Guadalcanal.

November 1942. Japanese counter-attacks against United States forces in the central Solomon Islands terminate in failure.

November 1943. United States and New Zealand forces establish beach-head at Torokina and consolidate the isolation of the Japanese forces on Bougainville-Buka.

October-December 1944. Australia taken over occupation of Torokin a from Japanese forces on Bougainville-Buka.

August 1943. The Japanese forces surrender.

March 1946. Australian civil Administration is re-established on Bougainville-Buka.

During the twenty-six months between the German attack on Poland and the Japanese attack on Pearl Harbor, life on Bougainville-Buka went on much as before. A few of the younger Australians in the islands left for home to enlist, and a small detachment of Australian soldiers was posted at Buka Passage to guard the air-strip being built there, but for the rest of the population, indigenous and expatriate, the European war was a very remote and irrelevant affair, or was not thought about at all. Locally, the most important event concerning the approaching Pacific war was the setting ip of an intelligence network involving a handful of resident expatriates.

After World War I the royal Australian Navy devised a plan for reporting the appearance of unusual sea- and aircraft among the islands north and east of Australia, and in September 1939 the plan was put into effect. coast-watchers, as they came to be called, were appointed at strategic points along the chain of islands, from the Admiralties to the New Hebrides. They were supplied with tele-radios and a simple code, and were linked with naval headquarters in the south through the island centres of Rabaul, Port Moresby and Tulagi. At the beginning most coast-watches went civilians - chiefly planters, traders, and Administration officials - but in time they were given naval ranks.

The coast-watchers of Bougainville were a remarkable breed of men. for months or years during the war they lived in the island's interior keeping watch over enemy ship and plane movements, cut off from to her Europeans except by radio and an occasional air drop of supplies, existing under conditions of extreme physical privation, supported by some indigenes but turned against by others, and in constant danger of capture and death. To a degree that few other individuals can claim, they contributed to Allied victories in the Solomon campaigns. And though they were not there for that express purpose, their presence in enemy-occupied areas for months or years after the flight or evacuation of most other Europeans, provided evidence, if any Bougainvillain wanted it, that Australia had not wholly abandoned the two islands tot he the Japanese.

At the beginning of the Pacific war, coast-watchers were deployed at several key observation spots on Bougainville-Buka; at Kessa, Buka Passage, Inus plantation, Numanuma plantation, Kieta, and Toimanapu plantation. The heroic exploits of those who managed to survive sickness and capture will be recounted. Soon after Pearl Harbor, most of the non-official white residents were evacuated to Australia. Of the white missionaries, however, the two Methodists on duty remained, as did all the Marists priest, brothers and nuns.

Then, in late January after the Japanese had captured Rabaul and had begun to reconnoitre Bougainville-Buka by air, the D.O. (District Officer, the top Administrative officer of the Bougainville Districts, along with his staff and most of the remaining white civilians of east

Bougainville, commandeered a small mission ketch and made for Port Moresby. Those still remaining were a few soldiers, coast-watchers in the territory then serving indentures on local plantations or employed by the Admninistrat6ion). The cynicism and bitterness provided among Bougainvillians by this flight and 'abandonment' have endured ever since.

During March 1942 Japanese ships called at Buka and north Bougainville, killed an elderly planter suspected of spying, and captured two other whites - a Marist priest and the sole remaining Methodist missionary. (The latter, along with 1100 other persons, were eventually lost at sea in the Montevideo Maru, which was torpedoed by a United States submarine while en route to Japan. On 30 March Japanese forces landed and occupied Buka Passage and Shortland Island and shortly thereafter the Buin coast as well. Meanwhile the surviving coast-watchers and the small army detachment had established their bases inland and were reporting on enemy dispositions and movements.

The army detachment, twenty-five men trained as commandos, was led by Lieutenant J.H. Mackie. The coast-watchers, W.J. Reed, assistant district officer at Buka Passage, and P.E. Mason, the proprietor of Inus plantation, by now held naval rank. From their observation points -

Reed overlooking Buka Passage and Mason overlooking first Kieta and then Buin and the Shortland Islands - these two were able to observe and report Japanese movements from Rabaul and Buka towards the north and central Solomon Islands, a contribution of immense value to the Allies' subsequent Solomon campaigns.

Marist Bishop Thomas Wade's decision to keep his mission members at their various posts was based partly on a tradition 'that did not disdain martyrdom', and partly on the hopeful belief that the Japanese would deal tolerantly with non-combatant missionaries. For a while this hope was realized, but as time passed and Japanese reverses in the Solomon Islands increased, more and more restrictions were imposed upon the Marists, including internment and worse.

At the beginning of the occupation the Japanese forces adopted friendly, even fraternal, attitudes toward the Bougainvillians, presenting themselves as their deliverers from white oppression and as ethnic cousins and partners in the glorious new Co-prosperity Sphere. On Buka, where contact was earliest and closest, schools were set up to teach Japanese language, customs and songs. Indigenous officials were presented with Japanese titles and impressive new insignia, and were frequently consulted. The populace was encouraged to revive the ceremonial veneration of their ancestors.

There and elsewhere the invaders were at first scrupulous in their bartering for food and payment for labour, and the molesting of indigenous women was firmly and effectively forbidden. Also, on Buka at least, the Japanese deliberately sought to win over the affections of the population at large by a show of friendly egalitarianism. Visitors were hospitably welcomed at the military camps, and friendship between soldiers and indigenes was encouraged.

The initial reactions of the Bougainvillians to these events differed widely. On Buka the Japanese were at first ceremoniously welcomed by much of the populace. For the devotees of the cargo cults, the flight of the whites and the immense resources of the newcomers spelled fulfilment of the former cult leaders' promises. This was reinforced by the Japanese, who deliberately encouraged ancestor worship, through which it was considered that Christianity would be weakened and a bridge provided to Japanese State Shinto. Even non-cargoists and adamant anti-cargoists were seemingly impressed with the newcomers' military might. Knowing only what they saw, it must have struck them as highly unlikely that whites would ever again return to become their masters.

Belief in continued Japanese mastery was also promoted around Kieta by the statements of some Marist clerics of German nationality, but this was offset somewhat by their (American) bishop; though pro-Allied in sentiment, he insisted for pastoral reasons upon his missionaries' neutrality. Kieta had also been the scene of looting just after the precipitate exodus of the Administration officials, but coast-watcher Reed hurried there from the north and managed to restore Administration authority, which lasted until the Japanese occupied the site.

Elsewhere on Bougainville Island during the first half of 1942, the indigenes had only sporadic contact with the Japanese, or no contact at all, and their attitudes towards whites and Japanese seemed to have varied according to their own individual pre-war relations with the former. some of them gave heroic proof of their loyalties to a specific missionary pastor or former employer, while others evidently delighted in the discomfiture of some or all whites. And even those without commitment to one side or the other were realists enough to accept the new order, since it appeared destined to remain.

On 7 August 1942, United States forces attacked and captured Tulagi and established a beached on Guadalcanal. during the following words the Japanese counter-attacked with large numbers of ships and planes from their bases in the north, but by mid-November the counter-attack was called off, in failure. The part played by the Bougainville coast-watchers in this crucial Japanese setback can hardly be overestimated. As wave after wave of Japanese aircraft flew south to destroy the exposed United States bases and the unloading, sitting-duck supply ships, they were spotted and reported by the coast-watchers in time to permit fighter planes to meet and down most of them before they reached their targets.

Japanese ships carrying supplies and reinforcements were similarly spotted and met the same fate. To the coast-watchers and most other remaining whites the turn of events was welcome indication of an eventual Allied victory, but it led the Japanese to the strengthening of their defensive forces on Bougainville and Buika. Buin was built up into a major land base, and several other posts were established or reinforced around the islands' coasts. Whether the ordinary Japanese soldier or sailor viewed these developments as hopeful or otherwise is not reported. for the Bougainvillians themselves - except possibly those close enough to Europeans to share their perspectives - the Japanese defeat on Guadalcanal was either unknown or uncomprehended, and was outweighed by the visible local evidence of increased Japanese strength.

With their entrenchment on Bougainville-Buka, the Japanese also adopted a sterner attitude towards the remaining whites. The missionaries were increasingly restrict5ed in their activities, until the point was reached when some were taken captive and others, including the bishop, led fugitive lives. Patrols began to harry the coast-watchers, but these jungle-wise veterans were able to elude them and continue with their work. As for the islands' Chinese settlers, some had long since been interned and others sought refuge in the jungle.

The larger Japanese presence, and their more active efforts to turn the indigenes against all whites, were accompanied by some change in Bougainvillians' behaviour towards the opposing alien sides. Throughout the larger island the coast-watchers and fugitive whites began to be treated by the indigenes with indifference or unfriendliness' in some places the latter actively sided with the Japanese as spies or guides.

This mood of hostility was most evident around Kieta, where bands of coastal villagers calling themselves 'Black Dogs' conducted murderous raids against inland, and presumably neutral, villages, and joined with the Japanese to hunt down fugitive whites and Chinese. Lest one be disposed to blame the Japanese overmuch for actively enlisting the Bougainvillians' assistance in that non-indigenous conflict, it should be pointed out that the coast-watchers did not hesitate to execute indigenes who endangered their own activities by aiding the Japanese.

On Buka, Japanese efforts to Nipponize the indigenes continued until the end of 1943. The schools they established proved attractive to young people and quite successful in inculcating anti-Allied sentiment. After a while, when Allied military success began to reduce the flow of supplies, more and more demands were made by the Japanese on the indigenes for labour and garden produce, but this was done in the name of shared sacrifice against a common enemy. These demands took some of the bloom off the Buka Islanders' earlier enthusiasm for their new masters, but evidently did not dispose them more favourably towards their former ones.

Under the pressure of Nipponization and general anti-white sentiment, Christianity undoubtedly suffered a relapse on Buka. but if the pagan leaders of the local cargo cult had hoped to profit by this, they were to be disappointed. As described earlier, the initial appearance, and for awhile the movement flourished widely and publicly. But for reasons that are not clear this florescence did not endure. According to some reports it was actively suppressed by the Japanese, who beheaded three cult leaders who were about to kill one of their opponents as a human sacrifice to the cult's guardian spirits.

Another more credible interpretation of these executions - which did in fact occur - is that the victims were suspected of pro-Allied behaviour at a time when Allied air attacks were increasing.

During the early months of 1943, the position of the Japanese forces on Bougainville-Buka worsened through shortages and increasing air attacks from the Allies. The lot of the remaining Europeans and Chinese became correspondingly perilous, and more and more indigenes turned from friendliness to indifference, or from indifference to hostility towards them. by June nearly all the non-military whites and some of the Chinese had been evacuated by US submarine. Even the stout-hearted Marist bishop, Thomas Wade, was finally persuaded, or rather commanded, to depart, leaving only those members of his order who were unable or unwilling to escape. finally, in July, the surviving coast-watchers were evacuated, their existence having become so imperilled by more aggressive Japanese patrolling and increasingly hostile indigenes that they were unable to carry on their reporting; moreover, by this time the Allied forces had moved so much closer that coast-watching was no longer as useful.

On 1 November 1943, United States forces landed at Torokina, on Bougainville's west coast, and quickly established there a beachhead of fifty square kilometres. The purpose of the manouevres was not to conquer the Japanese in direct combat, but to isolat4e and neutralize them still further, while using the base for intensified air attacks against the major Japanese concentration at Rabaul. somewhat later these measures were reinforced by the Allied occupation of Nissan Island to the north of Buka, and by beachheads on New Britain itself, so that the Japanese on Bougainville-Buka were effectively cut off from all outside help and left to 'die on the vine'. The dying on that particular vine turned out to be slow and tragic affair.

When the Americans landed At Torokina there were an estimated 65,000 Japanese on Bougainville-Buka, the major concentration being at Buin and around Buka Passage, with smaller detachments at places along the east coast and strategic points in the interior. In March 1944, the Japanese mounted a determined counter-attack against the United States base at Torokina, but when that failed and the Americans gave no sign of attempting to enlarge the base, the Japanese settled down, the more hopeful of them to await supplies and reinforcements, the more realistic to stay alive until the war's end.

In October 1944, Australian forces with some New Zealand reinforcements were sent to Torokina to relieve the Americans, who were destined for other missions in islands nearer Japan. by this time the Japanese forces had been reduced in number to about 37,000 to

40,000, some 25,000 to 28,000 having died during the American's eleven-month stay there. About 8000 died in combat and twice that number from sickness and starvation. In fact, by the end of 1944, with large-scale military encounters on the islands at a virtual standstill, hunger had become the Japanese garrison's principal foe.

In an effort to replenish their diminishing food supplies, the Japanese planted large gardens near their bases, and requisitioned more and more of the indigenes' own food. In addition to depriving the latter of their existing stocks, these measures reduced their already scarce stable land and, through conscription, took away labour needed for growing their own food. To fend off starvation at some of the smaller bases, the Japanese resorted on occasion to raiding indigenous gardens; and instances were reported - difficult to authenticate but circumstantially credible - of desperate Japanese soldiers resorting to cannibalism.

The Bougainvillians' reactions to all these events varied from place to place. In the vicinity of the larger Japanese bases, in Buin and around Buka Passage, they had no recourse but to remain hungry and nurse their resentments in silence. In other places they actively resisted the Japanese, with bloodshed on both sides. Some of those most caught up in this new phase of the war managed to find refuge within the

Allied perimeter at Torokina, where they were fed and housed and, if able-bodied, given jobs. In more remote mountain areas, out of reach of both Japanese and Allies, the war continued to be the cause of some deprivation in terms of trade goods and money-earning opportunities; but that was all.

For reasons which appear to have included national pride and military zeal, the Australians decided in December 1944 to break out of the Torokina beachhead and reconquer Bougainville-Buka without waiting for the war to be brought to an inevitably successful end elsewhere. Since this decision was widely criticized at the time and publicly condemned after the war, it requires no further discussion here, except to note that it also surprised and puzzled the Japanese commanders on the islands. Realizing their predicament, and being neither more nor less courageous than soldiers elsewhere, they apparently would have been content to live and let live unless forced to defend themselves. A similar attitude was evidently held by many of the Australians involved in the campaigns, but as the record shows they did not let their doubts and reservations curb their actions when called upon to fight.

The progress of the ensuing major campaigns are indicated in Figure 10. Not shown, however, are the movements and encounters of the various Australian guerrilla parties which reconnoitred and harassed Japanese outposts and patrols from perambulatory inland camps. Leaders of these parties included two experience-hardened pre-war residents of Bougainville, Paul Mason of coast-watching fame and Norman Sandford of Numanuma plantation. The epic adventures of these guerrilla parties and their indigenous supporters provided weighty evidence of the measure of sacrifice and heroism of which Bougainvillians were capable once their loyalties were mobilized.

When Japan's capitulation brought an end to these campaigns in August 1945, the Australian forces had captured most of the smaller Japanese bases and were preparing for the final assault on the major base in Buin. by the time Australian casualties numbered 2088: 516 killed or dead of wounds, and 1572 wounded. On the other side, 8500 Japanese were killed during the Australian occupation and another 9800 died of illness. No figures have been p0ublished concerning the total number of casualties suffered by the Bougainvillians themselves in these campaigns, or in direct consequences of any other phase of this calamitous war, the causes and objectives of which most of them did not even comprehend.

Full civil government was restored in March 1946; that is to say, the civilian Australian administrators resumed control of the islanders' lives after an interim of more than five years of military control. What effects did the events of the war years have upon the Bougainvilllians themselves? As was just noted there are no wholly reliable statistics available describing the numbers killed or wounded as a direct or indirect result of the war. They were undoubtedly high, but probably not nearly so high as of those who died from war-induced illness, from starvation, fatigue and lack of medical services. (During the early phase of their occupation, however, the Japanese are reported to have provided fairly good medical care for their indigenous neighbours.)

The effect of the war on the Bougainvillians' material goods - their houses, gardens, groves, house-furnishings, tools, etc. - is difficult to assess, although some estimate may be given by the amount of the war-damage claims which were ultimately paid. In addition, one must include among their losses the almost total destruction suffered by pre-war buildings, both Administration and mission, which bound schools, churches and medical services. Nor can these losses be balanced by pointing to all the camp sites, roads, runways, etc., constructed on the islands during the war, since virtually none of these was of use to the post-war Bougainvillians.

However, despite the damages suffered in terms of life or limb, or physical deprivation or goods, the most far-reaching effects were probably psychological. Demographically, the population quickly resumed its tempo of rapid natural increase, and economically their homes were quickly rebuilt. But the changes undergone in the mental attitudes of some of them - towards whites and towards themselves - served to ensure that relations between the two would never again be as they were before the war.

The precipitate flight of most of the whites and the collapse of most white institutions at the beginning of the war must have led even the most unsophisticated of Bougainvillians to question the pre-war colonial status quo. The continued presence of the Marists long after most other whites had gone may have tempered somewhat the general disenchantment, but in the end most of the end most of the Marists had had to flee as well.

During the first year of the war the Japanese military superiority added disdain to the disenchantment felt by Bougainvillians towards their former Australian masters. In turn, the subsequent Japanese defeat may have led most indigenes to moderate these views somewhat (although the part played by the United States did not escape them); but the whole war experience seems to have nourished a view among them that no colonial regime is necessarily perpetual.

The war also suggested to many that possession of a dark skin does not necessarily and inevitably require one to be treated, at worst as subhuman, and at beast as a well-meaning but ignorant child. The early Japanese policy of fraternization encouraged this change in expectations, and it was probably reinforced by the subsequent behaviour of United States and Australian troops, some of whom seemed to have promoted it actively and deliberately. If those new views of colonialism and ethnic relation had been limited to the Bougainvillians alone, they probably would have been forgotten in time' but they were shared with vast numbers of people elsewhere, and thus began to exert a dominant influence over Bougainvillians' post-war lives.

The Post-War Era

For most Boutgainvillians the period from the end of World War II to the middle of 1964 was one of gradual and only moderately unfamiliar change. The basis for most of that change lay in the new post-war policies adopted by the Australian government towards its Territories of Papua and northeast New guinea. In fact, those policies began to be formulated during the war, when the Labor government decided to make native welfare the principal objective in governing those territories, in deed as well as in word. This change of emphasis was of course in line with Labor's traditional ideology and in tune with anti-colonists stirrings elsewhere. but it was reinforced by a renewed recognition of the strategic military importance of New guinea to Australia's security, and by the corollary that a more prosperous, better educated, and politically sophisticated indigenous populatin would provide a stronger shield against future aggression from the north or the west.

In this spirit an agreement was made in 1946 with the newly federal United Nations which gave Australia exclusive trusteeship over the former Mandated Territory of New Guinea (Papua was already on integral dependency of the commonwealth), subject only to the obligations that administration would be carried out so that 'the customs and usages of the indigenous inhabitants would be protected, their cultural and educational advancement assured, their rights and interests safe-guarded, and an increasingly progressive shre4 in the administrative and other services given to them, as the territory developed.

Meanwhile the Australian government declared its intention of combining Papua and the Trust Territory of New Guinea for administrative purposes, a practical arrangement that had been in effect since the early days of the war. This move was opposed by some members of the United Nations on the grounds that it might slow down the Trust Territory's political development, or even lead to eventual Australian annexation of it. Despite those objections, Australia continued to administer Papua and the Trust Territory as a single dependency, but also continued to submit its reports to the United Nations covering the latter only.

A whole chapter would be required to trace how the war-born policy underwent change over the ensuing thirty years. Here in this brief account will be considered only the highlights of these changes, as background to the particular concern with Bougainville and Buka. In terms of official government policy concerning the future political status of the (combined) Territory of Papua and New Guinea, there were some major shifts. The first was towards a larger, ethnically balanced, measure of self-government for all the Territory's residents, then there was a move towards an emphasis on a government largely of and for indigenes; and finally towards an independent and mainly indigenous nation.

The move towards implementing the policy of ethnically balanced self-government began in 1949 with the setting up of a Territorial

Legislative Council. The inclusion of sixteen official members in this advisory body guaranteed that the Administration would retain firm control of it, but the addition of twelve non-official members, including three nominated indigenes and three members elected by the expatriate population, betokened some broadening of representation. It was the expatriate non-official members, and particularly the elected ones, who were most vocal in pressing for a larger share of self-government; the indigenous members tended to hew to the Administration's line.

Of course, 'self-government' meant different things to different people in those early post-war days. To many of the Territory's whites it meant more freedom to run their own enterprises without Canberra's bureaucratic control, and while this view of self-government may have included some sentiment for increased indigenous participation, it was based largely on concern for the interests of the whites themselves. As for the official Administration view of self-government, it was undoubtedly more pro-indigene in sentiment, but was constrained by the assumption that the indigenes' interest would be better served by withholding political power from them until they could be educated to make the 'right' kinds of decisions for themselves.

As for the larger issue of independence, the Minister for Territories, Paul Hasluck, told the Australian Parliament in 1960:

> We are not going out of the Territory in a hurry. In our judgment of the situation as it exists today, the Territory will need our help for many years to come and the advanced leaders of the indigenous people say strongly that they need us for a long time ahead. We are not going to abandon them or our own people who are working with them.

Nevertheless, events elsewhere moved the Administration speed up whatever timetable it may have been following regarding both self-government and independence. Thus, in June 1960, after this return from a Commonwealth prime ministers' conference, the (Liberal Party) Prime Minister, Robert Menzies, made the following statement:

> Whereas at one time many of us might have thought it was better to go slowly in granting independence so that all conditions existed for a wise exercise of self-government, I think the prevailing school of thought today is that if in doubt you go sooner, not later. I belong to that school of thought myself now, though I didn't once. But I have seen enough in recent years to satisfy me that even though some independences may have been premature, they have at least been achieved with goodwill . . .

Another such event was a resolution adopted by the United Nations' Trusteeship Council in June 1960, calling on Australia to set target dates with respect to political, economic, social and educational development 'so as to create as soon as possible favourable conditions for the attachment of self-government or independence'. The government was also stipulated to faster action by events in adjoining West anew guinea, where an Indonesian government was moving to take over control from the Dutch. And finally, many indigenes were themselves beginning to express a desire for a larger share in their own governance, and this sentiment received influential support from some Administration officials.

In response to these and other pressures the government set up a new Legislative Council in 1961 containing a majority of non-official members, including twelve elected members. The most noteworthy action of this new body, which contained six elected indigenes, was to foster the development of a much-enlarged and more widely representative successes to itself. This latter body, the House of Assembly, scheduled for 1964, was intended to provide the Territory's indigenes, with a larger share in their government, including education in responsible citizenship, while ensuring the continuation of the Territory's political stability and economic growth.

With this in mind, the new body was to include ten official members appointed by the Administrator, and fifty-four members elected by universal adult suffrage (males and females eighteen years of age and over). To choose the elected members, the Territory was divided into forty-four open electorates and ten larger special electorates; candidacy in the former was open to any adult resident regardless of race, but only non-indigenes, i.e. whites or Chinese, could be candidates in the latter. Equality of population size was the main criterion in establishing boundaries for the open electorates, but this was outweight4ed somewhat in an effort to conform to ethnic, geographic and administrative boundaries as well. Thus the smallest open electorate, Manus, contained a population of only 18,000, while the largest, Bougainville District (Bougainville, Buka, Nissan, etc.), contained 54,000.

The Mine

The gold fever that gripped the mainland New Guinea in the 1920s and 1930s spread to Bougainville as well, where small quantities of gold and traces of copper were discovered in the mountains behind Kieta. Beginning in 1934 a gold mine was operated at Kupei, but on such a small scale that it was regarded by most European residents as a pathetic pipe-dream: by the time the Japanese invasion ended its operation, only about 1789 ounces of gold and 80 ounces of silver had been extracted from it. After World War II traces of alluvial gold were discovered in the mountains west of Kupei, but only a few attempts were made to extract it.

In 1960 a geologist of the Australian Bureau of Mine Resources, Geology and Geophysics re-examined the country around Kupei and confirmed the presence of intensive low-grade copper mineralization. Again, this would have been dismissed as nothing more than a scientifically 'interesting' discovery but for certain current developments elsewhere. At the start of the 1960s, disparate developments around the world combined to produce the possibility of profitable large-scale mining on the island. Each by itself was unlikely to have achieved that; together, and with the foresight of some remarkable individuals, they changed low-grade mineralization on the island from a matter of academic geological interest to one of major risk investment.

A layman hesitates to assign priorities to these factors, which included new theories of ore genesis and novel techniques in geological exploration' new prospecting techniques, ranging from stream sampling for dissolved metal ions to innovative use of helicopters for both human and equipment transport in heavy jungle; technological breakthroughs in the scale of machinery, both for materials handling and for minerals concentration, and a worldwide market uncertainty about the future assured availability of copper as a vital industrial commodity.

In Australia, the vision of one mine executive from Broken Hill had already led to a series of new discoveries undreamed of twenty years earlier. Maurice Mawby had spent heavily on diversified risk exploration of the bauxite resources of Weipa in north Queensland, and for a token fee had operated for the Australian government the uranium mine at Rum Jungle in the Northern Territory. Another visionary, Canadian geologist Haddon King, began to envisage new theories of ore genesis: if you were right about how minerals became concentrated, the likelihood of finding economic mineralization was greatly improved.

Meanwhile, in the United Kingdom, an entrepreneurial financier, Val Duncan, began to create a world-size mining company on the tiny initial base of Rio Tinto, a rundown Spanish mine operated since the days of the Romans; Australia, and particularly uranium, became his chosen fields of opportunity. Australia had a stable and pro-development government, unlike those of mineral-rich countries in Africa and Latin America which wee then in the process of decolonization and nationalization. In due course Duncan's Rio Tinto merged with the London-based mining house consolidated Zinc (created by L.B. Robinson) to form RTZ in London and CRA in Melbourne, with Mawby at its head.

Would entrepreneurial flair, geological foresight and a pro-development Australian overseer have automatically led to mineral development to Papua New Guinea? It was 'at best highly improbable' without the other factors of technology and world demand. World demand went through a turbulent decade, as forced nationalizations of major producers such as those of Chile and Zambia caused fears of involuntary or deliberate restrictions of supply. In addition, prices on metal exchanges for copper were fluctuating; as a result, several developing countries formed the Conseil Internationale des Pays of d'Exportation de Cuivre, or CIPEC, the attempted copper equivalent of oil's OPEC.

While all those events were taking place, new technology in material handling and scale of metallurgical concentration made remarkable advances in economies of scale. the visible growth of ore trucks from a carrying capacity of 50 tonnes to 170 and then 210 tonnes was only the outward manifestation of this. New techniques and skills were also developed in planting of open pits, in size of ball mills, and in production scheduling.

The consequence of those technological innovations was that, given a large enough ore resource to justify the investment over years, huge quantities of mineralized rock at 1 per cent copper or less became mineable, where a generation earlier the 'cut-off grade' which divides economic ore and waste had been perhaps 4 per cent. In a true sense, technology created new reserves. In Australia and elsewhere, this dramatic increase in the ability to mine and process low-grade ore profitably extended across the whole field of minerals commodities, not simply to copper ore.

So, were technology and demand the extra determining factors? Again, 'not so'. In 1960, RTZ and CRA were entrepreneurial but not cash-rich miners. The Panguna deposit had no 'cap' or 'pod' of high-grade gold which might have paid for a modest self-financing start. Neither the Australian government nor Australian banks were willing financial backers of larger minerals projects in their own homeland, let alone in a UN Trust Territory. International banks, sensitive of the disruptive nationalizations taking place elsewhere in what was coming to be called the 'third world', were also unenthusiastic about risk in a not yet independent nation and in the fluctuations of copper prices.

The final necessary element was the ability to have in place - long before even final production details were firmly settled - a system which would make both the high capital cost and the proposed output from a probable mine securely 'bankable' in the eyes of lenders. That might not have been achieved at all except for independent feasibility studies and for innovatory international marketing of a new financial concept, namely, that long-term contracts for supply of premium copper concentrate to smelter firms in Japan, Germany and elsewhere in Europe, could be a financeable prudent risk. In 1960 almost no Australian mining engineers, even the most experienced, had themselves much more than seen operation on this scale.

The Australian tradition, of which Mawby was a part, was then centred on underground mining of relatively high-value ore. The experts in the new skills of large-scale open-pit mining and large-scale metallurgy were mostly North American, as were the bulk of the relevant lending banks. In consequence, American expatriates joined Australians in the initial top management level of these new ventures in Papua New guinea, just as they did in similar ventures in Australia and elsewhere. It was transfer of technology on a giant scale.

In 1968, exploratory drilling and road-making were already on a huge scale by South Pacific standards. It was as hard for anybody as for other non-miners to conceive that the activity was only a 'project' supported by risk capital, and neither a proved deposit nor as yet a financeable mine. The new economics of scale imposed their own stern disciplines. both the exploration companies and the potential lenders crunched members ever many months - a 'small' mine on low-grade ore was simply not possible.

Indeed, even the mining and treating of 30,000 tonnes a day, which the original plan envisaged, was calculated to be insufficient for profitable operations. A very costly and extensive exploratory drilling programme had to be undertaken in order to produce forecasts large enough (80,000 tonnes a day) to repay the borrowings needed to finance the operation, given the expected fluctuations in the world price of copper over a ten-year period. In the course of that exploration the most promising area was found to be in the Panguna Valley.

After eight years of exploration, evaluation, and construction, mining began there in April 1972 and continued, probably, until May 19898, when hostile actions by some local residents forced it to that shut down. During its seventeen years of operation this mine was the largest industrial enterprise in Papua New guinea in a number of respects, including especially its production of national revenue. It produced and shipped to overseas buyers concentrate containing nearly three million tonnes of copper, 304,412 kilograms of gold, and 780,875 kilograms of silver, for a net sales revenue of about 1900 million kina.

Up to the end of 1988 a total of some K685 million had been paid to the Territorial, later national, Papua New guinea governments in direct taxation, customs duties, retail sales taxes, and withholding taxes on dividends; plus another K166 million in dividends on shares owned by the government. Altogether, these sums constituted an average of about 17 per cent of the government's internal revenues, and the overseas sales of the ore concentrates amounted to about 40-50 per cent of the nation's foreign earnings.

In addition, the new country received as early as 1967 (long before leases were granted) an unparalleled 'free trade' into what was to become its largest single industry, source of finance, and exporter. The miners offered the Administration 20 per cent of equity in the development at par (rather than the much higher price later offered to other investors). Australia took up the offer much later when the project's viability was established. This acquisition passed to the new country almost unnoticed with the other transfers of decolonization, As D. S. Carruthers and D.C. Vernon wrote in 1990:

Given the CRA was taking all of the risks on exploration and feasibility, this was an offer unprecedented in mining projects in underdeveloped countries, and to the authors' knowledge, but still not been matched voluntarily by any other company anywhere in the world.

Moreover, up to the closing of the mine the company had paid about K75 million to the government of the North Solomon Province in royalties and taxes, plus another K22 million to Bougainvillian landowners in the form of royalties, rent and compensation. these figures do not include the monies paid by the mining company to the Administration in the form of rents, etc., not the amounts paid by the company to Papua New Guinea residents in dividends, nor the income taxes paid to the Administration by company employees.

The number of individuals employed by the company and its contractors varied over the years. During the exploration and evaluation phase it was in the hundreds; during the construction phase it reached more than ten thousand. since the beginning of mining the number averaged about four thousand, of which about 80 per cent were indigenous Papua New Guineans. How much of the salaries and wages of those employees remained in Papua New

Guinea is impossible to discover, but it cannot be ignored when judging the economic impact of the mine, particularly on Bougainville.

Members of five district Bougainville ethnic (i.e. language-cultural) units resided in the region directly affected by the mine. Of them a large majority were Nasioi, and most of these were rural villagers engaged in subsistence farming and some cash-cropping of cocoa. Although mainly 'rural' in lifestyle, most of these Nasioi were well acquainted with the local colonial institution and with many individual Europeans. As will be recalled, it was along this region's eastern coast where Europeans first settled: first the Catholic mission, in 1904; next, colonial officials, German and then Australian; then Australian planters and Chinese merchants; then a detachment of Japanese and finally a return of all of the pre-war types of outsiders - officials, planters, merchants and missionaries.

Individuals among the region's Nassioi doubtless differed to the content and degree of their Westernization and in their attitudes towards outsiders, but their contacts with persons and things Western were on the average far more frequent than those experienced by most other Bougainvillians, including most other Nasioi.

The second of Bougainville's native peoples to experience the direct impact of mining activities were the Austronesian-speaking

Rorovanans, it will be recalled, were descendants of fleets of Shortland Islanders who had 'colonized' - seized and settled on - this coastal area in the nineteenth century and had remained ethnically 'intact' ever since. They appear to have adjusted more comfortably to the immediately adjacent Europeans than had their Nasioi neighbours. By the mid-1960s the nearby village of Uruava (Arawa) was more Nasioi than Uruavan. As related earlier, when this writer was on Bougainville in 1938-9 the residents of this village still spoke the Austronesian language of their ancestors, who like the Rorovanans had migrated here from Shortland Island, but a century or so earlier. by the mid-1960s, however, intermarriage with the neighbouring Nasioi had led to the near-extinction of the Uruava language, along with many other Uruavan customs.

The fourth set of Bougainvillians to be directly affected by the mine were those of the Nagovisi people who resided west of Panguna along the southern borders of what was to become the mine's tailings. The fifth were a community of Austronesian-speaking Banoni, whose small coastal village near the outlet of the Jaba River had to be moved to avoid flooding by that tailings-widened stream. Now to unravel the corporate transformations undergone by the company that discovered, developed, and operated the mine.

The Consolidated Zinc Comapny Ltd of London (CZC) owned the Zinc Corporation Ltd of Broken Hill, Australia, and had a managing interest in new Broken Hill Consolidated. In 1962 it merged with the Rio Tinto company Ltd to form the Rio Tinto-Zinc Corporation Ltd (RTZ). At the same time, in Australia, Consolidated Zinc Proprietary, a wholly owned subsidiary of CZC, merged with Rio Tinto Mining Company of Australia Ltd to form Conzinc Riotinto of Australia (CRA). To reduce this (incestuous!) genealogy to its essentials: London-based RTZ owned 85 per cent of Australia-based CRA in April 1965.

When it was decided that CRA would undertake a systematic search for copper deposits in the Southwest Pacific, New Broken Hill Consolidated Ltd joined with it as a junior partner, and it was this combination that launched the exploration on Bougainville in the form of an entity, named CRA Exploration (CRAE), which was created for that and other mineral searches in the southwest Pacific. (Among other facilities, (CRAE possessed the Craestar, a former Japanese tuna-fishing vessel, fitted out with a laboratory, a helicopter landing deck, and accommodation for an exploration party of ten.)

After CRAE's exploration had turned up promising prospects on Bougainville, the work of evaluation was handed over to yet another new entry. Bougainville Copper Pty Ltd, which was a subsidiary of

Bougainville Mining Ltd. Then, after the commencement of mining, in 1972, the company was registered in the Territory of Papua and New Guinea and renamed Bougainville-Copper Ltd (BCL) - which, it has remained ever since. In the account that follows, all these transformation will be simplified by referring to the organization as either the company of BCL. The governmental entities which initially regulated the exploration and over all Papua and New guinea matters, including those of Bougainville, rested with the Australian government in Canberra, and specifically the Minister for Territories.

The Bureau of Mineral Resources, Geology and Geophysics played a role in copper search throughout Australia, and its regional geologist stationed in Port Moresby and visited Bopugainville in 1960 and found porphyry-type copper mineralization there, but the bureau did not follow up this lead.

The Territory's Administrator in Port Moresby was of course subordinate to Canberra, but could, and often did, propose and administer minor changes in policy, including changes regulating mining. In port Moresby the mine company's principal contacts were with the Assistant Administrator, Economic Affairs, and the Department of Lands, Surveys, and Mines. On Bougainville, the company's main governmental contact for the first few years was with the Assistant District Officer (later, commissioner), stationed at Kieta, the District Officer being headquartered at Buka Passage at that time.

In 1966 a Mining Warden's Court was set up in Kieta to adjudicate complaints ('plants') against the company for damage to property. In 1969 a new office was set up, the Chief Liaison Office in the Bougainville District, charged with overseeing all relations between the company and residents of Bougainville. also in 1969, the Public Solicitor's Office based in Port Moresby began to be more deeply involved in relations between the company and Bougainvillians; it actively championed the latter's definitions of their rights and claims, taking out writs against the Administration itself, and pursuing litigation up to Australia's High Court.

Another governmental personality closely concerned with the mine in its early years was the Hon. (later Sir) Paul Lapun, Bougainville District's first member in the Territory's House of Assembly. In addition to the entities just listed, during the early years of its operations the company had some relations with members of some of Bougainville District's local government councils, including those of the Kieta Council, but those elected officials had very limited functions and authorities, and the institutions themselves did not last long.

Individual Catholic clergymen have played influential roles in the company's relations with Bougainvillians from start to present.

A few have been silent or neutral, but many have been vocally against the company, some loudly and effectively so. they have not only championed Bougainvillians' claims for larger shares of company revenues, but also denounced the mine's effects on the physical environment and on public morality. Moreover, some of the most influential Bougainvillians with whom the company dealt over the years had been trained in Catholic schools, some of whom had reached, and later left, the priesthood.

Other players on the Bougainville scene during the early years of the company were the island's plantation managers and merchants - the former mostly Europeans, the latter mostly Chinese. By the late 1980s nearly all of the former had left, after selling off their properties. Even while still there, few of them had much to do with the company, except to experience increasing difficulties in recruiting and keeping their workers in the face of the company's higher wages and more 'interesting' jobs. As for the merchants, the increased in the sales receipts in the early days of mining diminished when company-sponsored supermarkets opened in Aarawa and Pangua.

Bougainville island

Bougainville Beyond Being

Bougainville's close contact with the outside world and its integration into Papua New Guinea are recent. The first permanent Christian mission and first colonial administrative post (under German New Guinea) were established in 1901 and 1905 respectively. Relations were often troubled between Bougainville and central colonial authorities (German New Guinea to 1914, Australian-administered New Guinea from 1914 to 1946, with an interlude of Japanese Army control from 1942 to 1945, and Australian-administered Territory of Papua and New Guinea from 1946 to 1975). Bougainville attempted to secede only days before Papua New Guinea's independence. The situation was resolved only by constitutional changes guaranteeing autonomy for Bougainville under a provincial government system.

The pattern, however, continued after Papua New Guinea became independent from Australia in 1975. The conflict that began in 1988 prompted the closure of one of the world's largest copper and gold mines, operated at Panguna in central Bougainville from 1972 to 1989. The mine, together with widespread plantation and small-holder cocoa production, had made Bougainville Papua New Guinea's wealthiest province. But for most rural communities, patterns of considerable isolation and autonomy were changing only slowly in the 1980s. Most people continued to rely heavily on subsistence agriculture.

From independence to 1990, Bougainville had its own relatively effective provincial government and a local government system. But the state structure in Papua New Guinea—including Bougainville—was weak at all levels; it often failed to impose policies on local communities determined to oppose them.

Conflict and Peace

While the Panguna mine was the major contributor to Papua New Guinea's GDP and government revenue, its perceived imposition by the colonial regime for the benefit of the rest of Papua New Guinea was widely resented in Bougainville, and from the mid-1960s contributed to an already emerging ethno-nationalist movement for secession from Papua New Guinea. Bougainville attempted secession through a unilateral declaration of independence in 1975, the dispute being settled by Papua New Guinea establishing a constitutionally based system of decentralization from 1977.

In 1988, localized disputes over impacts of the mine and the revenue share received by younger landowners sparked violent conflict. Papua New Guinea police responded to destruction of mine property with widespread violence that was the catalyst for the mobilization of a wider ethno-nationalist rebellion built on a long history of grievances and resistance.

Separation from Papua New Guinea became the central goal of a rapidly escalating rebellion. Most non- Bougainvilleans left Bougainville during 1989 and early 1990, many fearing for their lives in a process that was in some respects a form of ethnic cleansing.

After Papua New Guinea forces withdrew from Bougainville following a March ceasefire, Bougainville declared independence in May 1990 in a unilateral declaration that gained no international recognition. Intra-Bougainville conflict developed from the early 1990s, complicating the rebels' efforts.

A series of peace-making endeavors ended the conflict in 1997. Long and complex negotiations aimed at resolving both intra-Bougainville tensions and those between Papua New Guinea and Bougainville resulted in the political settlement of August 2001.

Among the goals for an independent Bougainville fought for by the Bougainville Revolutionary Army (BRA) was autonomy for customary social groupings. The BRA also sought to strengthen these groupings as well as Bougainville state structures by building close links between the two. Such goals remained central to the Bougainvillean agendas; a political settlement with Papua New Guinea in the Bougainville Peace Agreement of August 30, 2001 guaranteed them a high level of autonomy. The settlement kept open the possibility of independence through a constitutionally guaranteed referendum on the subject, to be held among Bougainvilleans 10 to 15 years after the first autonomous government is established.

Almost all senior Bougainville leaders see the process of building linkages between customary and state power as crucial to developing sustainable state structures for Bougainville—whether they be those of an autonomous Bougainville government or of an independent Bougainville.

The Impacts of Change

As elsewhere in Melanesia, the impacts of colonial and post-colonial change on the preexisting social structures in Bougainville have been immense. A wide range of new ideologies were introduced, as were new arenas for power competition: the Christian missions, the colonial administration, cooperatives and companies, elected local-level governments, village courts, and the elected provincial government. Challenges arose to traditional understandings of the world and how it worked, and new sources of identity emerged.

Undoubtedly, Bougainvilleans were relatively powerless in relation to the force of colonialism, but they were not simply swamped by change imposed on them. While there is ample evidence of resentment and resistance, many people welcomed change, seeking and often finding personal or group advantage from it. In the process, customary social structures and their associated traditions were altered.

Yet customary social structures--including customary authority--in many ways remained strong and vibrant. In particular, customary authority remained important to decision-making and dispute resolution. Many rural communities, for example, dealt with criminal offenses internally. Those dissatisfied with the decisions of traditional authority, however, were able to engage in "forum shopping," taking matters to the police or to village courts.

Identity and Separatism

During the 20 years following World War II, Bougainvilleans increasingly expressed grievances about racist treatment by "whites" as well as colonial neglect resulting in limited infrastructure and economic development.

From the late 1960s the most important grievances related to the copper mine. Residents most resented the influx of thousands of outsiders from elsewhere in Papua New Guinea who, they felt, disrespected Bougainville cultures, squatted on customary land, and competed for economic opportunities that Bougainvilleans regarded as rightfully theirs. The distribution of mine revenues--both between the Papua New Guinea government and Bougainville and within the Bougainville lineages whose land was leased for mining-related purposes--was also seen as unfair.

Efforts to come to terms with the outside world included various forms of resistance to colonial rule, among which were the "cargo cults," evident even before World War II and continuing even today. Cargo cults probably originated in beliefs widespread in pre-colonial Melanesia about a millenium when all good things would be available. In the colonial era such cults were also a reaction to what was seen as the inexplicable injustice of the affluence of whites. They were most likely influenced by Christian missionary promises about the afterlife. The cargo cults involved Bougainvilleans' assertion of autonomy over their communities and lives.

Resistance was also evident in different movements emerging after World War II, the best known being the Hahalis Welfare Society (Hahalis) in Buka, which for several years from the late 1950s sought to develop its own path toward the economic advancement of its 6,000 members and many sympathizers. A mixture of customary and "modern" forms of organization, Hahalis refused to participate in the colonial elected local government system, opposed integration of Bougainville into Papua New Guinea, and criticized the Catholic Mission for failing to assist people's material advancement. Confrontations with police riot squads, followed by mass prosecutions, ensued. Concern about the impact of Hahalis resulted in development projects for Buka, and greater interest by the Catholic Church in material progress and social justice for its adherents.

Hahalis had links with similar movements. Notable among these was a group in the mountains of central Bougainville that remains active today: Damien Dameng's Me'ekamui Onoring Pontoku (roughly translated from the Nasioi language as "government of the guardians of the sacred land"). Often called the "Fifty Toea Movement" (a reference to the monetary contributions members made), it was often dismissed as an ill-informed cargo cult, but was in fact rather different.

Dameng and his supporters believed that customary social structures and ways were being undermined by the outside world. From around 1959, Dameng built support among several thousand people around ideas of rebuilding customary social structures. In the process, however, they built something new, rejecting "bad" aspects of custom, and building in some "good" aspects of the changes brought by the missions and the colonial administration.

The movement's adherents, however, believed that their social structure was built mainly upon custom, and saw it as superior to the colonial administration and the Christian missions, both of which Dameng opposed. His opposition extended to elected local-level governments, to Bougainville's provincial government, and to the services these governments provided, including formal education.

Dameng's opposition to the damaging impacts of the outside world also extended to the Panguna mine. He believed it destroyed land (the basis for social relations), introduced cash payment for use of land (thereby undermining Bougainvilleans' relatively egalitarian customary social organization), and brought in large numbers of outsiders. These earlier forms of resistance were linked with a broader separatist movement emerging at least as early as the late 1950s that opposed the BCL copper mine and supported Bougainville's separation from

Papua New Guinea. The continuity is illustrated by Dameng's position within the coalition of Bougainville groups opposing the Papua New Guinea government during the conflict. Separatist support mobilized on the basis of identity, both in the lead-up to the attempted secession of 1975 and in the conflict from 1988 to 1997. The most distinctive marker of Bougainvillean identity was dark skin color. (Bougainvilleans tend to refer to the lighter-skinned people of other parts of Papua New Guinea by the pejorative term "red-skins.")

Pan-Bougainville identity was itself probably a product of colonialism, originating perhaps in a sense of superiority on the part of domestics and security personnel on German colonial plantations over people from other parts of New Guinea. This identity was reinforced by geography--the concentration of a relatively homogenous but distinctive population in a defined area remote from the rest of Papua New Guinea and closely linked to the Solomon Islands.

Commentary on Bougainville often presents Bougainvilleans as a united people, resisting colonialism, mines, and, later, Papua New Guinea. In fact, sentiments about grievances, resistance, and separatism varied considerably throughout Bougainville, probably reflecting differences in language, culture, length and intensity of colonial contact, and economic status. Separatist support has generally been weaker in Buka and in the north of the main island of Bougainville, the areas with earliest colonial contact and consequential advantages in terms of education and access to economic opportunities. Such differences were important among the complex factors contributing to intra-Bougainville conflict between 1988 and 1997.

The Importance of Custom

By the mid-1980s, increasing intensity of participation in the cash economy gave rise to new kinds of disputes that traditional leaders were not well-equipped to deal with. The increasing availability of education, together with new forms of economic activity and increasing mobility, reduced social cohesiveness, and young people were less willing to accept customary authority and limits on behavior.

Bougainvilleans believed that customary social structures were threatened by the disinterest of the youth, the election of persons other than chiefs as local government members and village court magistrates, and the continuing influx of outsiders. Bougainvilleans also saw increasing crime, especially, but not only, in urban areas, as a symptom of social disintegration.

In response, Bougainvilleans proposed reducing the number of outsiders by returning the unemployed and squatters to their home provinces elsewhere in Papua New Guinea and transforming elected local level governments into councils of chiefs. Public concern and debate about such issues undoubtedly impacted the early stages of the conflict, especially the pressure on outsiders to leave Bougainville, and enhanced the status of customary authority and customary ways during the period of the conflict.

During the conflict, especially in areas where all forms of government authority had ceased (the whole of Bougainville and Buka for most of 1990 and most of Bougainville for the early 1990s, as well as much of Central and South Bougainville until the late 1990s), the absence of alternative forums enhanced traditional leaders' status. Communities relied more on customary social organization and customary authority for general decision-making and dispute resolution.

The BRA and its associated civilian government (the Bougainville Interim Government, or BIG) established in April 1990 sought to build local administration and dispute settlement procedures upon customary authority. From 1991, a three-tiered system of councils of chiefs (COCs)--clan, village, and area councils--was established in many areas. The COCs dealt with administrative matters and disputes at their own levels, and the higher level COCs could review decisions of lower levels.

The COCs were, of course, not customary organizations, but they included customary leaders who applied, as best they could, customary norms, and so were generally understood to be strengthening custom, by their very existence and through the norms they applied. It was not just a matter of adapting custom; in some ways, it was also a matter of reviving it. For example, in part of southwest Bougainville, the identity of the "chiefs" was not readily apparent. It was finally agreed that they must be the people at the end of the "rivers of pigs" distributed in certain kinds of ceremonial exchanges, and those so identified were expected to exercise customary authority through the COCs. In general, the work of the COCs in most areas was well regarded within the community.

In 1996, Theodore Miriung, the premier of Bougainville's provincial government (which had been suspended in 1990 but was reestablished in 1995), developed a modified version of the COC. Miriung had earlier been involved in establishing the COCs, and considered strengthened social structures necessary to a restored social cohesion. The new bodies, called councils of elders (COEs), were set up under provincial government law to cover people from culturally coherent areas.

The people of a COE area were empowered to choose whether to select their representatives by election or by custom. COEs were to be the basic unit of administration and of judicial power, and the basis for bottom-up planning. Miriung envisioned COEs providing the basis for a symbiotic relationship between customary authority and state authority. Basing the state on customary authority would enhance its legitimacy, and exercising state powers would enhance the stature of customary leaders. On the other hand, Miriung recognized that customary authority was essentially autocratic and might only be viable as a transitional measure over perhaps 10 to 15 years, by which time economic and social change could be expected to create pressure for a more democratic system of government. It was in part for this reason that the COE legislation gave communities the right to choose, at five-year intervals, whether to select COE members by custom or through elections.

COEs now operate in most parts of Bougainville. Their performance has so far been uneven, for many reasons. Some COEs are far too large, and remote from the communities they serve. For example, one of the largest, the Leitana COE, serves the whole of Buka Island, more than 30,000 people, and has become deeply involved in Bougainville-wide politics rather than staying focused on the many Buka communities. The COE system lacks adequate administrative support from the provincial government, due partly to the government's ongoing financial crisis, and partly to the political leadership's focus on negotiating future arrangements rather than on consolidating existing structures.

As "normalcy" has returned to various parts of Bougainville, and as their stature has diminished, chiefs are no longer an almost unchallenged source of authority.

Future Governance in Bougainville

Under the autonomy arrangements agreed to in the Bougainville Peace Agreement, Bougainville has wide power to establish its own institutions. While the original leader of the 1988 rebellion, Francis Ona, has not yet joined the process, most other Bougainville leaders--including Damien Dameng, who, in his early seventies, continues to lead Me'ekamui Onoring Pontoku--support it.

Most people agree that a new Bougainville government should be based on customary authority. Processes for drafting a constitution for an autonomous Bougainville, expected to begin this year, are likely to involve wide public consultation. But discussion has thus far been limited to the strengthening of the COE system and the possibility of establishing of a bicameral legislature involving an upper house representing chiefs.

A range of difficulties, both practical and fundamental, confronts the enterprise. The practical difficulties have already limited the effective implementation of the COE system in Bougainville. More fundamental issues involve challenge to customary authority; rapid economic and social change will only exacerbate the problem. Resolving the tension involved in basing an accountable democratic system of governance for an autonomous or independent Bougainville on what is in many respects an autocratic system of customary power will not be easy. There is also potential for tension between conceptions of individual rights and responsibilities and the rights and responsibilities of groups, though of course Bougainville will not be the first place to deal with such tensions, and could learn much from experiences elsewhere. Discrimination by powerful local leaders against outsiders, both people from elsewhere in Bougainville and people from other parts of PNG, is also a threat.

These and similar potential problems should not be unmanageable, however, especially if effective and sensitive support and guidance is provided to customary authorities exercising new forms of power. Bougainvilleans are committed to the enterprise, and will undoubtedly bring great energy to it. They do not have a static view of their own custom. They want to build on it, and in so doing, to enable their multiple communities to find their own paths into an unpredictable future.

Bougainville Struggle: independence and the mine

It was a conflict that dominated the news in Australia during the late 1980s and '90s. The people of Bougainville were aggrieved; their land had been taken, exploited and destroyed. The repercussions still echo as the island holds elections in the lead up to a referendum on independence from Papua New Guinea

The story of Bougainville begins in the dying days of Australia's colonial presence in what would soon become the independent nation of Papua New Guinea. Bougainville, as well as the rest of what would become PNG, came under Australian control after World War II.

During the '60s, as independence approached, there was debate over whether or not Bougainville would be part of the new nation. The island is the largest in the Solomon Islands archipelago and its people have more in common in terms of ethnic, tribal and customary values with Solomon Islanders than with PNG.

'Bougainvilleans are a united group with a sense of a separate identity, centred particularly on their very dark skin colour, much darker than the average in the rest of Papua New Guinea,' says Anthony Regan, a constitutional lawyer at ANU and an advisor to the current Bougainville government.

'During the post-war period, the beginnings of a linking of political and economic demands to Bougainville identity asserted against the rest of Papua New Guinea began to emerge. Even in the early '60s when a UN mission visited Bougainville, there was a call from some Bougainvilleans for the UN to take over or for Bougainville to be part of America. I'm not saying this was every Bougainvillean but there was a significant element of dissatisfaction.'

That feeling of dissatisfaction intensified with the establishment of what would become the world's largest open cut copper mine at Panguna. The Bougainville Copper Agreement was struck between a company then known as Conzinc Rio Tinto of Australia and the Australian government in 1967 and the mine began production in 1972, three years before PNG independence.

'Many of the local people were opposed to the mine,' says Griffith University's Professor Ciaran O'Faircheallaigh, who went to Bougainville as a PhD student during the '70s to look at the impact of the deal. 'At different points, the colonial administration had to bring in riot police to suppress opposition to the mine. We're talking about a situation in which many people didn't want the mine, it was forced on them by the colonial administration through a law, the Bougainville Copper Agreement, in which they had no say.

'Another very big problem was loss of land associated with the project. One of the major protests was at a place called Rorovana, where women were heavily involved in a protest over the building of a port and other facilities. They were removed by the riot police and some of them were jailed. Similarly, at the mine site itself people were losing their land, people were being relocated to other areas where there often wasn't garden land available. They were being moved on to other people's customary land. Remember, the livelihoods of all these people depended entirely on their land.'

Moreover, the mine caused tremendous environmental damage, according to O'Faircheallaigh.

'Mining companies were allowed to simply dump the waste into the rivers, which is what happened. There was no tailings dam in the way there would be in Australia to confine these. About 50 million tonnes of waste a year was simply dumped into the rivers, which became biologically dead within a couple of years. They broke their banks and the tailings and the waste from the mine started to spread out onto other people's land.'

The Panguna mine turned out to be incredibly profitable for CRA and its parent company Rio Tinto. So much so that CRA and Rio recovered their entire capital investment in just two and a half years. They were making huge sums of money out of the project, but the compensation that was paid to people was minimal, and often wasn't sufficient even to allow them to buy food to replace the productive land they had lost.

The Bougainville government, set up in 1977, officially got some royalties—about 5 million kina at the time, probably worth about US$40 million today. It was significant revenue, and the government and used it to try and build infrastructure and prosperity across Bougainville as a whole. Within Bougainville, however, there was a strong sense that the mine had been imposed mainly for the benefit of the independent state of Papua New Guinea, which received a much greater share of the royalties.

During the '80s, a new generation of landowners from the mine area were becoming adults. They had never received any of the compensation for the land taken. The size of the mine workforce had fallen from 10,000 during construction to about 3,500, and Bougainvilleans only occupied about 30 per cent of those positions. By the mid-1980s, young people from all over Bougainville were increasingly resentful about the lack of employment opportunities.

Young landowners and mine workers, discovering that they couldn't get their concerns heard by the PNG government or the company, decided to take action. They began destroying mine property, burning buildings and blowing up power pylons. Instead of trying to address their grievances, both the Bougainville government and the national government called in police mobile squads from elsewhere in PNG. Using violence to try to suppress opposition to the mine simply drove more people to join the young rebels, however.

The mine was shut down in May 1989 and has never reopened. PNG troops left Bougainville in March 1990 in the lead up to intended peace negotiations. Police pulled out as well, and suddenly the Bougainville Revolutionary Army led by Francis Ona was in charge of Bougainville

'Very rapidly from mid-1990 the situation descended into highly localised conflicts, some of it over theft, some of it over payback of old scores, some of it about hitting people who had been regarded as supporting the Papua New Guinea government,' says ANU's Anthony Regan.

'It very rapidly then descended into an internal civil war in Bougainville, with very strongly pro-secessionist BRA people opposed by what were often former BRA who had been losing out in localised conflict who then sought the return of the Papua New Guinea forces.'

'It was ultimately, from 1990 through to 1997 when the conflict ended, a sort of dual-headed civil war, one between secessionists and Papua New Guinea, another between secessionists in Bougainville and anti-secession Bougainvilleans, and those two civil wars were masking a myriad of the local conflicts—very, very local, probably 70, 80 localised conflicts that had nothing to do with ideology, nothing to do with secession, all to do with land and local history and identities and so on. So it was a very tragic outcome.'

During the conflict, approximately 15,000 to 20,000 Bougainvilleans died. It ended in 2000 after seven years of protracted negotiations that involved New Zealand, Australia and the United Nations. A peace agreement was signed in 2001 by PNG and Bougainville. Both sides agreed that Bougainville would for the moment remain part of PNG but be allowed much more autonomy than other provinces.

Given the island's history, mining is a very sensitive issue and one part of the peace agreement was that the Bougainville government would ultimately take control of mining on the island. In March this year, that process was completed with the passage of the Bougainville Mining Act.

Mining in Bougainville is now completely controlled by the Autonomous Bougainville Government, whereas in every other province of PNG it's still controlled by the national government. The legislation also states, possibly for the first time ever, that minerals are not owned by the state, but rather by the customary landowners of the land under which they sit.

The final component of the peace agreement was that between 2015 and 2020 there would be a referendum in which Bougainvilleans would decide whether to remain part of PNG or become independent. PNG is not bound to accept the results of that referendum, but the referendum must be held at some point during that period.

Both the independence referendum and the possible reopening of the Panguna mine have been potent issues during the current Bougainvillean presidential and parliamentary elections.

'They are the two big issues,' says Anthony Regan. 'But there is a general view in Bougainville amongst the leadership and amongst very many Bougainvilleans that it's going to be very difficult to have either real autonomy or independence without mining. The Bougainville budget at the moment is about 350 million kina, roughly $150 million, but Bougainville-derived revenue is about 30 million kina, about $12 million.

'Bougainville, though, is still divided on the issue of mining. There are some landowners in the area very concerned about the reopening of mining, and there are others very worried about the possible environmental effects. So the issue is yet to be determined, but under legislation passed by the Bougainville government in March, Bougainville landowners have been given rights of veto over either exploration or development. So the Bougainville government's been saying from day one there will be no reopening of the Panguna mine if the landowners don't want it. And with the veto, the landowners will have the final say.'

'The Bougainville government would prefer to have the Panguna mine move ahead quickly if possible, if the landowners want it, mainly because it could be up and running within five, six, seven years, and generating significant revenue for the government even in the two or three years of construction, whereas in general in PNG, new mines from exploration to beginning of operation can take between 15 and 30 years. With the timetable for the referendum, a referendum being required by 2020, the government feels torn and under considerable pressure.'

The formal announcement of the results of the election is scheduled for June 8, but it is dependent on the speed of vote counting.

Victor Ross

The People, Culture, Tradition and Festivals
Reeds Festival

Culture is the main catalyst for unity amongst Bougainvilleans

It varies region-wide and has significant similarities that suggest a common migratory history.

Bougainville is mostly matrilineal with a minority of scattered patrilyneal communities in the Southern Region of Bougainville.

Clanship arrangements are unarguable the Eagles Clan (Manu), Roosters (Nakarip) and the Dogs (Nakas). Other clans of the likes are Hornbills (Kokomo), Cockatoos and others are defectors of the three main clans.

Chieftainship of a clan is chronologically inherited from women chiefs while the men provide patronage.

The Clan's male Chiefs always make decisions harmoniously with the intention to protect the integrity of the women who are the owners of land, property and traditional landmarks, hunting/fishing zones.

There exist three chiefs in a clan, one being the decision maker, the other being the warrior and the last as the messenger.

Barter system is still being practiced in most remote parts of the region.

Featured on the provincial flag is a tall hat, known as Upei. The Upei is a headdress worn by young men at their initiation and marriage ceremonies

Our descent to Bougainville was slowly opening the stunning views over the crystal clear blue waters and giving us a taste of what is to come. Our feelings were probably much close to those of the French explorer Louis de Bougainville, who has first discovered this beautiful volcanic island about 250 years ago and has named it for himself.

Despite its location in the remote corner of Papua New Guinea, the name of Bougainville is widely known. Even those thinking Papua New Guinea is an African country confusing it with Guinea in the West Africa, have heard about Bougainville war for independence, better known as Bougainville Conflict, the largest conflict in Oceania since the end of World War II. But Bougainville is also known for its unique culture and traditions, which have much in common with its close neighbour, the Solomon Islands.

Arriving in Buka, we were greeted with large smiles of the friendly charcoal-faced locals looking as if they have rubbed oily black paint into their skin. Although people from Bougainville look very different from the natives of other provinces in Papua New Guinea, they have something in common. They all share their unconditional love for buai, or betel nut, which grow in giant sizes in Bougainville, the highly praised "Buka buai".

Having attended Papua New Guinea festivals in the Highlands on several occasions, with the tribes distinguished by colourful and eye-catching costumes and body paint, and huge headdresses made with the birds' feathers, here, in Bougainville, we found a very distinctive traditional attire.

The Reeds Festival originated as a way to display and protect the vibrant and unique culture of Bougainville.
The support from sponsors, passionate about the PNG culture, made the Reeds Festival a regular bi-annual event held over two days in Arawa town, in the south of Bougainville island. The venue, located near the beachfront, has beautiful views of Pokpok Island, or Crocodile

island, the name given to the island due to its shape in the form of a large crocodile. The name pokpok is derived from the Papua New Guinea Tok Pisin word for crocodile – pukpuk.

The name "Reeds" Festival comes from the reeds, the bamboo panpipes used as a musical instrument. The reeds are the unique style in making music, which is practiced in the villages of Bougainville as well as in the Solomon Islands for ceremonial and ritual occasions.

Attending the Bougainville Reeds festival is a great way to see the traditional attire of Bougainville people.

Gone are those days, when people were wandering around in grass skirts. Nowadays, you won't see people dressed in traditional clothes on a daily basis. Although the locals eagerly adapted the Western style clothes, for special occasions, such as the Reeds Festival, they don their most beautiful traditional costumes.

The Papua New Guinea festivals are always a colourful affaire. Traditional clothing in Bougainville is very similar to the one found in the Solomon Islands, which isn't surprising given the proximity of the islands. The common attire is grass skirts and tapa cloth made from tree bark and dyed with natural colours. Traditionally, both men and women leave the upper body unclothed and cover only the lower body and the thighs, and decorate themselves with different kinds of traditional jewellery such as necklaces, belts, armbands, and hairbands.

String Bags, called Bilums, are also part of the costume. On a daily, the bilums are used basis to carry everything, from firewood to babies. If in the Highlands region of Papua New Guinea, the bilums are now often made of wool-based bright and colourful yarns, the bilums in Bougainville are still made using woven plant reeds.

The Bougainville Reeds Festival is the unique opportunity to experience the diverse culture of the island as it attracts the performing groups from all over Bougainville.

Bougainville possesses a unique and rich culture, which is kept alive in the form of ceremonies and elaborate rituals still performed today for such important events as birth, death, marriage, tribe reconciliation and young boys' initiation.

The people of Papua New Guinea are ethnically Melanesian but the country is home to more than 800 tribes characterised by their own distinct cultures and languages. With its 23 languages spoken throughout Bougainville, the island possesses a wide range of tribes, and the culture varies from region to region.

If for tourists, the Reeds Festival, with its dancing and singing, is a great opportunity to experience Bougainville rich culture, for young

Bougainvilleans the festival is the opportunity to learn about their culture and be part of the performing groups. Hopefully, having the younger generation interested in its origins, the unique culture of Bougainville will survive.

If the locals coming to the festival will find their extended family or friends to chat and exchange gossips, the tourists will find beautiful handcraft for sale – various kinds of bilums, hand-made jewellery, pottery etc.

At the time, when traditional cultures are rapidly declining worldwide, the festivals, such as the Bougainville Reeds Festival, provide a way to conserve the traditions for future generations. More importantly, they preserve the culture, something that makes us all unique – our differences.

www.ingramcontent.com/pod-product-compliance
Lightning Source LLC
Chambersburg PA
CBHW021100080526
44587CB00010B/312